S0-AGW-494

7
WEALTH
BUILDING
SECRETS

DE'ANDRE SALTER

To Teri,
I believe God with you
for the legacy of your
family.

Dylan...

7 WEALTH BUILDING SECRETS
Copyright ©2015 by De'Andre Salter

Unless otherwise noted, all Scripture quotations are taken
from the Holy Bible, New King James Version. Copyright ©
1982 by Thomas Nelson, Inc. Used by permission.

Scripture quotations marked CEV are taken from the
Holy Bible, Contemporary English Version. Copyright ©
1995 by American Bible Society. Used by permission.

Scripture quotations marked NCV are taken from
the Holy Bible, New Century Version. Copyright © 2005
by Thomas Nelson, Inc. Used by permission.

Scripture quotations marked NIV are taken from
the Holy Bible, New International Version. Copyright ©
Copyright © 1973, 1984, 2011 by Biblica, Inc.
Used by permission.

All rights reserved. No part of this publication
may be reproduced, stored in a retrieval system, or
transmitted in any form by means electronic, mechanical,
photocopying, recording or otherwise, except for the
inclusion of brief quotations in a review, without
prior permission in writing from the publisher.

ISBN: 978-1-939779-10-6 (Paperback)
ISBN: 978-1-939779-22-9 (EPUB)

Published by
LifeBridge
BOOKS
P.O. Box 49428
Charlotte, NC 28277

DEDICATION

This book is dedicated to my family, for releasing me to pursue God in a new way. Especially my wife Terri, who has mesmerized me since the first time I laid eyes on her across the lunch room in eighth grade at Saint Ann school in Newark, New Jersey.

And to my parents, Sam and Emma, who provided me with the entrepreneurial and Holy Ghost-filled DNA that has contributed to my success. I thank you.

I also dedicate this book to my father in the Gospel, Bishop Kenneth Ulmer, who has taught me to honor the place where I stand. In addition, special thanks to Bishop Sheridan McDaniel, Dr. Terrence Autry, Dr. Lydia Waters, and Pastor Bryan Carter, who provided me with positive criticism to sharpen my words.

3

CONTENTS

INTRODUCTION

Unless you were born with a silver spoon in your mouth, you probably know what it's like to be stressed out over money. Perhaps you've been handed a pink slip, received a dreaded call from a bill collector, or have stood for hours in an unemployment line.

Congratulations! Consider yourself fortunate that this book has found its way into your hands. You're about to discover what it means to have financial peace.

If you are of the opinion that having more money will solve all your problems, you're reading the wrong book. This has nothing to do with hitting a Powerball or Mega Millions jackpot. It's not even about receiving an unexpected promotion or a double bonus at work. I recently read a statistic that 78 percent of the National Football League millionaires retire broke.[1] So obviously, money is not the answer.

If God opened up the windows of heaven and showered down on you more money than you had room to receive, what would you do with your heavenly windfall? Would you use your newfound wealth just to acquire more 'stuff' or jet away to exotic foreign lands? Well, hang on. I'm about to show you another path—and it's not a short term fix or a treasure map that will lead you to instant riches. No, it's far more valuable. The Bible reveals seven wealth building secrets, and when you embrace them they will revolutionize your today and transform your tomorrow.

I don't think I'm overreaching when I say that just about everyone wants to be wealthy.

There is hardly a magazine or television news show that does not allocate at least 25 percent of its attention to wealth topics. In fact, there are entire networks dedicated to money management, finance, and the market.

The religious are not excluded from the discussion. I would estimate that every minister is doing some preaching, teaching, or small group discussion on money or wealth related topics.

If they are not, then the pews are probably getting emptier since money matters may be the #1 life issue of most congregants. According to University of California Berkeley researcher Gabriel Zucman, about half of the country has zero net worth. Therefore, the lack of financial resources is an issue for all races, most neighborhoods, all faiths, and pretty much every socio-economic group outside of the 1%.

In this book I offer a very unique perspective on the topic of wealth building, and it has everything to do with my background.

First, I wasn't born rich, but to rather meager means, in a hard working blue collar family, so I understand the issue of lack intimately.

Second, I worked my way to the top ranks of the insurance industry and then launched a successful entrepreneurial insurance brokerage firm, so I understand how true wealth is generated and know how to live in abundance.

Third, I am a pastor with theological training, so I understand how to read the Bible for its financial applications toward the goal of offering practical solutions to the number one problem of people in the pews—the lack of wealth.

In fact, when I am often asked about the secret to my success, my answer is the same for faith and non-faith audiences—my path has been directed by the application of biblical principles. You see, it is my belief that the Bible is not only for our eternal enrichment but it is written for us to learn how to live our best life in the here and now as well. Yes, the Bible is both a sacred religious book and one of wisdom.

I know this raises a red flag for some, that I speak of using the Bible in this manner, since there have been prior abuses. But, I am adamant that as a Christian entrepreneur, the wealth wisdom in the Bible has provided me with principles that unlocked abundance. To many earnest people, any use of the Bible's wealth wisdom is labeled, in my opinion, unfairly. In fact, the church and the popular media has been somewhat on a witch hunt for a particular brand of preaching called the "prosperity Gospel," which they say rebrands the Scriptures as a means for achieving personal wealth and success, which Jesus wants us to have.

Many of the faithful have allowed the "prosperity" wing of the church to highjack the biblical idea of abundance, but for me there is no denying that God is also a God of wealth. The Bible tells us, *"The silver is Mine, and the Gold is Mine"* (Haggai 2:8). No one should be afraid to preach, teach, and experience this truth.

I fully understand that the excesses of certain pastors and their ministries are often under attack —and in many cases, rightly so. While it may seem convenient to throw the baby out with the bathwater and say that the Bible is not to be used to understand and study wealth, it is impossible to do so without first removing over 2,300 verses in Scripture centered on the topic of wealth and money management.[2]

From my point of view, this is clear evidence that omnipotent God knew of a day where it would be very expensive to live and that we would need plenty of financial resources just to maintain a basic lifestyle.

I reside in the state of New Jersey, where the poverty line is nearly $40,000, double the national average of $20,000.[3] In other words, if you live in my region, money will most likely create your greatest stress and be the pressure that ignites new anxiety and crisis—and I suspect it is the same in most other areas.

Regardless of how many men and women criticize the rich, their secret sin is that they long to be wealthy too. Why? Because they live in America, where being poor is no fun.

The secular person's solution is to just work harder—hustling and hoping they can wave goodbye to poverty. The Christian response is to sow a seed, speak a positive confession, and pray money suddenly appears, because that's what the preacher told them to do. The problem is that secularists have a slim chance of rising out of poverty and keeping what they acquire because they have no spiritual foundation, which may lead them to an emptiness that money can't solve. Likewise, the Christian with limited or poor theology is in the same boat, since they have been taught to only *sow* more and *believe* more; in doing so, something is missing and they remain impoverished.

So, what is the solution? I believe the best path to abundance is from the inside out. Meaning, a person who is whole in his inner man can handle and manage unlimited wealth on the outside. Please read this carefully; without a strong moral and ethical foundation for wealth, one quickly faces destruction. All the prosperity in the world cannot make one happy inside.

This is one of the central financial themes that run through the Bible. There are countless warnings about the abuses of money, usury, and the results of financial greed. God has always been trying to tell His creation how to gain and manage wealth, and I will share some of those secrets with you in this book.

To me, the solution lies in understanding and applying divine principles—including the seven secrets you will find on these pages.

11

In this book you will discover how every person from the pew to the pulpit can move beyond positive thinking, speaking, and sowing, and reach the place where they are creating and reaping.

Secret by secret, I want to share how you can rebuild yourself into what I call a 'Christian wealth-making machine'— so that God's kingdom will benefit from your riches in a way that will make our heavenly Father smile. It is my goal that we create an army of prosperous believers who will honor the covenant God made with Abraham, and use such wealth to establish His kingdom on the earth.

I pray what you will find written in this book will turn your life around—as it has mine and the countless lay people, entrepreneurs, and tent-making pastors I have been blessed to coach.

Prayerfully, open your mind, soul, and spirit to *7 Wealth Building Secrets.*

– De'Andre Salter

ENTER THE CYCLE OF WEALTH

LIKE A HIGHWAY DESIGNED BY GOD, THE CYCLE OF WEALTH HAS MANY ENTRANCE RAMPS WHICH LEAD TO ABUNDANCE AND MANY EXIT RAMPS TO LACK

There are hundreds of so-called professional financial gurus who have devised formulas and paths that supposedly lead to prosperity, but the first secret of God's wealth building program may surprise you. It is not about moving from point to point on either a horizontal or vertical line. It's just the opposite.

Think of it this way: God created a world—and it was round. So it is only natural that when the Almighty set into motion a system of abundance it appeared as a circle. I call it *The Cycle of Wealth.*

This cycle is like a highway designed by God that has many exits and entrance ramps. There is always an opportunity for us to enter abundance and exit to lack by our behaviors.

It is a divine principle that whenever I complete a kingdom cycle there is wealth. But when I stray outside the cycle, I enter an orbit of poverty that affects both me and my family. This book is your new wealth building GPS; it will make you aware of particular entrances and exits, so you can avoid going the wrong route.

Together, let's look at the three phases of the cycle of wealth. I am deliberately using the words *"supposed to,"* in these descriptions because, even though God designs something, He created each of us with a free will to walk away from His ordained plan.

Phase #1: We are supposed to be born into an inheritance.

Mankind, being the children of the Creator, inherited the earth after it was formed. We did no work to create it or earn it; it was given to us by God. While we will develop this concept further later on, for now, let's accept that mankind was born into an inheritance from his Creator and, likewise, we should flow in that same manner—that our creations (children) likewise are *supposed* to be born into an inheritance.

We were created to live without lack, and I will prove this using the first chapter of Genesis.

Take a close look at what the Bible says concerning the first family: *"Let Us make man in Our image, according to Our likeness; let them have dominion over the fish of the sea, over the birds of the air, and over the cattle, over all the earth and over every creeping thing that creeps on the earth"* (Genesis 1:26).

This is the first phase of the cycle: Adam was *born* into something that already existed. He personally didn't plant a tree, a flower, or grow the original garden. Remember, God made him from dirt and dust. But after the Creator breathed life into his being, he suddenly awoke into a world of plenty. This is called an inheritance—something you have not worked for or necessarily deserve.

Every man and woman is created in the same fashion.

Now let's take an even closer look at Genesis 1:28, which I believe reveals the wisdom of God and His heart for us to live in abundance and not poverty: *"Then God blessed them, and God said to them, 'Be fruitful and multiply; fill the earth and subdue it; have dominion over the fish of the sea, over the birds of the air, and over every living thing that moves on the earth.'"*

Before you read this verse too quickly, note the order in which God instructs man to build his life— first be fruitful and second multiply. There is a wisdom and an order which is intentional here, since if a man multiplies his life without first being fruitful, then he takes an exit ramp on the cycle of wealth and enters himself into the land of poverty. On the other hand, if a man first becomes fruitful, and then expands, he continues on the cycle of wealth and operates in abundance.

Guess what? God gives us the secret to wealth building or poverty building at creation—be fruitful in what you do first, and then multiply yourself. Why is this wise? Imagine this, you are born and given one apple as your inheritance? What should you do with it? If you get married, you have to share the one apple with your spouse. If you get married and have two children, that one apple will have to feed all four of you. At best, each of you must thrive and survive off of one measly apple. It would be virtually impossible to have any abundance except the abundance of debt that would be required to support the family.

But, imagine, you first eat part of the apple and remove it's seeds. Then you ration the apple to last you for a season while you plant the seeds in the ground. In time, you will have an apple tree with many apples. This, my friend, is God's definition of fruitfulness.

Now, with a wealth of apples, you can go find your spouse, have children, and enjoy plenty of apples to share, grow, and replant seeds for an orchard. This is God's view of multiplication. The idea of fruitfulness relates to bringing forth something from the original (mastery), while multiplication is the idea of expansion of the mastered thing.

There are many who are living in poverty simply because no one has taught them or told them that they should be fruitful in life before they attempt to replicate. The applications of God's order here are endless—from business expansion to personal wealth creation. In fact, many businesses and investment managers have sought to follow this exact science for eons—don't expand too fast, first master the model.

Let's turn to the whole concept of inheritance I am using here.

While I understand that Reformed/Evangelical theology usually interprets the garden as "marriage and family," there are additional views. In some Jewish commentaries, the Adam/Eve/garden imagery is a vision or preview of what God would do for Abraham Isaac, and Jacob, and ultimately with Israel—giving the land as an inheritance.

Moses, speaking on behalf of God, detailed that inheritance is the right of the firstborn (Deuteronomy 21:15-17). And since Adam was the firstborn, he must have a legacy as well. If not the garden, then what was it?

Even Jesus speaks of inheritance in respect to salvation (Matthew 19:29). As Christians, we believe redemption cannot be earned, but is something we receive and accept as the beneficiaries of Jesus' work on the cross, not ours. Likewise, Adam received the garden, a perfect place to be fruitful and multiply, but he did nothing to earn it; this was a benefit of God's work.

Adam and the garden can also be a type of Israel and the land. According to Genesis 1, the first man was meant to expand a holy progeny for God.

However, since Adam did not obey the Creator's instructions (will, rule, law) he lost the territory that was given to him and was exiled. In other words, Adam, took the first exit off the cycle of wealth.

Likewise, Israel, a holy nation formed by God and called out to bear the truth, was given a land full of milk and honey (a "Promised Land") to create a holy lineage that would obey God's will. Since they failed to live by the commandments of the Almighty, they eventually took a wealth exit and entered a season of lack.

Phase 2: We are supposed to gain something while we live.

The design for our life is to increase what God gave us. I'm not saying that we are all born with the same measure or amount of talent, skill, or ability, but from our individual starting point, we are to seek growth, development, and increase. This is not a prosperity principle; it is simply a principle of life!

Regardless of the interference from family, societal, or governmental factors, we are to add to what we were born with. Poverty should have no hold on our lives, and, as developed earlier, we have been given creation instructions on how to avoid it.

We see a picture of the intended gain in Genesis 2:15: *"Then the Lord God took the man and put him in the garden of Eden to tend and keep it."*

The Hebrew word for "tend" is *abad,* and it means to continually serve or work. Therefore, we are made to focus our lives on productivity and work for the purpose of gain and growth. Of course, life in the garden was from God, but growth of the garden depended on Adam's daily toil.

Then there is the Hebrew word for "keep" which is *shamar*, and it means to guard, observe or give heed, to have charge of or to be a watchman.

Therefore, God introduces man to the idea of stewardship. It was man's charge to make sure nothing destroyed the garden and the life therein. That charge remains for us today. We are to spend our days working and being productive, gaining from our starting place, all the while being good stewards of what we have been given and gained, so there is something to pass down.

Phase #3: We are supposed to leave something behind.

If we are not fruitful and there is no increase, it will be impossible to enter the third phase of the cycle: creating an estate.

The reason we must do this is so the next generation can be born into their own fruitful garden—so they can gain—enabling them to *also* leave something behind. This is the only way to establish a legacy and, generation by generation, remove the poverty noose from our necks

I pray your eyes are open to seeing this never-ending cycle. It is a far cry from the lottery mentality so many cling to: to pick six, and scratch off Jesus. What blessing is it for a person who wins a jackpot, but has no concept of how to use the resources for further gain? Without this knowledge, the cycle would be broken; the money lost, and there wouldn't be a penny left in their estate.

Because of the dismal deficit in which many find themselves, they want to cheat the system, skip ahead, and have it all *right now!* But this is not how wealth building principles operate.

Please take note. Adam was placed in the Garden of Eden with specific instructions to take care of it, so the abundant fruit would be available for his children and his children's children. It would be part of their estate.

However, there was one warning: *"Of every tree of the garden you may freely eat; but of the tree of the knowledge of good and evil you shall not eat, for in the day that you eat of it you shall surely die"* (verses 16-17).

The Almighty didn't sugar-coat His instructions. Everything He gave as an inheritance was theirs. All they had to do was to tend the garden, cause it to prosper, and pass it on to their heirs. However, when they disobeyed God's command, they took an exit ramp on the cycle of wealth the Lord had established and entered into a land of lack outside the garden.

Adam went from an inheritance and abundance to poverty and lack, because he was disobedient to the instructions given to him for his benefit. The poverty problem can be solved only by a commitment to following the instructions given to man to live in abundance on the earth.

RIDING WITH SOMEONE ELSE ON THE CYCLE OF WEALTH

While there is something to be said for a quiet ride alone, it is also so much more fun to sit back, relax and have a great driver take you to your destination. Imagine your driver knows where there is an unlimited amount of resources from which you can prosper? Why not join along for the ride, rather than trying to find it for yourself, with no map, no travel experience and no guidance? Picture Abraham as a driver on the cycle of wealth.

We certainly see this cycle positively operating in Abraham, but there are also some great lessons to be learned about entrance and exit ramps from examining the life of Abraham's nephew, Lot.

God came to Abraham in a faraway country and gave him these instructions: *"[Go] to a land that I will show you. I will make you a great nation; I will bless you and make your name great; and you shall be a blessing. I will bless those who bless you...and in you all the families of the earth shall be blessed"* (Genesis 12:1-3).

Wow! What an amazing promise! God was saying that not only would Abraham be favored, but anyone connected to him would also be blessed. Wealth creation often works this way. It is very typical for tech entrepreneurs to spend most of their time building relationships with mentors and financiers for two reasons: (1) to learn how to build a business and (2) to raise money for their dream. In other words, to get their new website or product to market, the smart ones accept the need for wealth building discipleship.

You must not miss the power of divine connections that are sent to help you unlock and guide you to the nearest entrance on the cycle of wealth.

Since disciples make disciples, we need to be mentored by those who live by proper stewardship principles and who have experienced financial break-throughs. Strong people can lead the weak to maturity, and financially savvy men and women can help us move from poverty to prosperity through the practice of apprenticeship and finding a role model.

As you continue reading the biblical account, not only did Abraham receive the inheritance God prom-ised, but so did his nephew, Lot, who journeyed with him when they left the plains of Ur of the Chaldees. Like the savvy tech entrepreneur, Lot also entered into Abraham's cycle of wealth—gaining from the associa-tion with his uncle.

Every time I think about this, it makes me realize how important it is that we surround ourselves and listen to those who are progressing financially, if we are to walk in abundance! Listening to destitute individuals talking about money is delusional! It would be very rare to learn calculus from an English teacher, or chemistry from a history professor. So if you want to know and understand wealth, find some-one who has achieved it—but be sure you make the distinction between a person who is just making money and one who is reaping abundance God's way.

At first, Lot had the right idea. He sat under instruction and received wisdom so he could learn how to replicate Abraham's cycle.

Scripture records that Abraham and Lot (by association) had been so favored that the land could hardly sustain all their cattle and herds. Abraham didn't want his nephew to venture out on his own, but yielded to his wishes and they decided to go different directions. Abraham told Lot, *"If you take the left, then I will go to the right; or, if you go to the right, then I will go left"* (Genesis 13:9).

What was Lot's choice? He saw an exit sign, the fertile plain of Jordan that was *"well watered everywhere (before the Lord destroyed Sodom and Gomorrah) like the garden of the Lord"* (verse 10). This is what he picked. Lot coveted the land with the greenest grass, or the 'quick fix.' By making this decision, however, he was about to exit the cycle of wealth.

Lot should have stayed under his uncle's mentoring; instead, he walked into a treacherous situation. The kings of Sodom and Gomorrah held him hostage and seized his resources. As a result, he entered into a cycle of poverty. Remember, every exit from the cycle of wealth is an entrance ramp onto a new highway, called the cycle of poverty.

There are millions today who fail to learn how to increase what God has blessed them with. Suddenly, they find themselves swerving onto an "off ramp" instead of staying on the road to abundance.

After Lot went his separate way, God made this amazing statement to Abraham:

> *Lift your eyes now and look from the place where you are—northward, southward, eastward, and westward; for all the land which you see I give to you and your descendants forever. And I will make your descendants as the dust of the earth; so that if a man could number the dust of the earth, then your descendants also could be numbered. Arise, walk in the land through its length and its width, for I give it to you* (verses 14-17).

It didn't make any difference what land Abraham picked, even if it was a scorched desert. God was going to bless him and he would gain even more.

PASSING ON ABUNDANCE VS LACK

As Abraham remained persistent in the wealth building cycle, a son, Isaac, was born. Because he had the birthright, he (unlike Lot) received Abraham's inheritance—and continued to gain and prosper. In fact, after Abraham died, God made this covenant with Isaac: *"Dwell in this land, and I will be with you and bless you; for to you and your descendants I give all these lands, and I will perform the oath which I swore to Abraham your father. And I will make your descendants multiply as the stars of heaven; I will give to your descendants all these lands; and in your seed all the nations of the earth shall be blessed"* (Genesis 26:3-4).

When a severe famine plagued the territory and everyone was pressing Isaac to relocate to Egypt, he remembered the covenant and told them, "Forget it! I'm not leaving!" In other words, Isaac understood the cycle and was not going to listen to others who did not.

The Bible records, *"Then Isaac sowed in that land, and reaped in the same year a hundredfold; and the Lord blessed him. The man began to prosper, and continued prospering until he became very prosperous; for he had possessions of flocks and possessions of herds and a great number of servants"* (verses 12-14).

Isaac became so financially rich that even the king grew jealous of his fortune. All this came about because he faithfully stayed in the cycle of wealth. First, through inheritance, second through gain, and Isaac also entered into phase three: leaving an estate.

When Isaac was nearing the end of his life, his major concern was providing for his children as his own father had done. He didn't want to leave those he loved burdened with debt.

WHAT BREAKS THE CYCLE OF WEALTH?

You may ask, "But what if I happened to be born into *nothing*—into a deficit situation? Where do I turn?"

While you may not have caused poverty, you can become impoverished through oppression, fraud, misfortune, persecution, judgment, even systems of government. As it is written, *"Like a roaring lion and a charging bear is a wicked ruler over poor people"* (Proverbs 28:15).

Without question, we can find ourselves in financial trouble because we don't have enough insurance to cover an unexpected illness or a house that burns to the ground.

As a pastor, one of the saddest, most painful moments is sitting with a mourning family who cannot pay for a funeral—a household led by a person who failed to realize the necessity of leaving something behind, or one who was born so deep in the poverty hole that he or she could never get themselves out.

Regardless of your financial situation, please do some advance planning, including making out a will and spending a few dollars for burial insurance. If you can't afford an attorney, at least write your wishes down on a piece of paper, have it notarized and put it in a safe place. And while we are on the topic, take the time to make a note as to what your funeral service should include—the color of flowers, the speakers, etc. Avoid having two cousins fighting over who's going to sing a rendition of *Amazing Grace!*

While there are certain things we cannot control, there are some causes of poverty that we *can*: laziness, neglect, a culture of impoverishment, and a "needy" mentality.

There is no time machine that allows us to go back in history to undo the injustices done to any of our ancestors which, without argument, clearly affected what each of us were born into. Instead, we need to look to the future and understand a wealthy man's way of thinking.

King Solomon, one of the richest men who ever lived, wrote: *"Laziness leads to poverty; hard work makes you rich"* (Proverbs 10:4 CEV). This is not idle speculation. It is a universal law of God—both in the spiritual and natural realms.

While usury has always existed in forms of slavery, apartheid, or other evil and corrupt labor systems, it remains a truth that the only way to achieve a proper wage or income is through the work of ones hands or mind. God made men to be industrious, giving Adam, as mentioned earlier, a primary assignment to work. Therefore, regardless of past or present abuses of labor, one must not lose hope that work provides the means for those of us not born into money. Wealth creation starts with work and flourishes when we are paying others to do the work for us.

Here's an unavoidable fact. Even if a lazy person is a trust-fund baby with rich parents, he can lose or squander his fortune. There are countless stories of people who inherit amazing riches, but because of their idleness, slowly, over time, they end up without a dime.

Such were the misfortunes of the Stroh family, whose empire at one time was valued at 9 billion dollars and now is worth very little.[1]

As I look back over my life, there were days when my bills were piling up so fast that I became severely depressed. One month, my paycheck was $500 short of my rent. The next year it was short the entire amount! That was before I decided to break the cycle of poverty and get back to the place God intended for me to live.

There is a Proverb that tells us, *"Great wealth can be a fortress, but poverty is no protection at all"* (Proverbs 10:15 CEV).

If you are underwater financially and nothing changes, you will set into motion a cycle of poverty that will become generational.

Back to the question: How do we move forward and experience gain? Let's face it. Just like Adam, all created beings have been blessed with the ability to overcome any scarcity. But we have to apply biblical principles concerning work and stewardship, and prayerfully make the right choices.

Remember these wealth building secrets:

- We are designed to prosper from the cycle of wealth.

- We are supposed to increase our lives, no matter the starting point.
- We are supposed to leave an estate behind for the next generation.
- If you want to be wealthy, become a wealth building disciple of those who are prosperous financially.
- Work! Prosperity is tied to industry.

LIGHTEN YOUR LOAD!

SOMETIMES YOU HAVE TO LOSE SHORT-TERM TO GAIN LONG-TERM

There are storms—and then there are storms! In this chapter I'm not referring to an overcast sky that causes a brief shower and then moves on. This is about the turbulent storms of life—financial, relational, emotional, physical—that hit you like a tornado. These are gales a mere umbrella won't solve.

Have you ever found yourself in such a financial situation that you were completely discombobulated? The kind that caught you so off guard that one moment your life was bright and sunny, and the next your skies were so dark that you couldn't see beyond the clouds?

Perhaps the problems struck like a burst of thunder so loud that you woke up in the middle of the night thinking it was the Rapture—and when you realized it wasn't true, you wished it was!

One minute you were whistling while you worked, the next minute you're laid off. One day they were sending you credit cards in the mail, now they're being canceled.

The howling winds of worry overwhelm you, and you cry out:

- "God, are you still there?"
- "God, do you even care?"
- "God, why me?"

The longer a financial crisis lasts, the more our hopes begin to fade. At first, you may have braced yourself and thought, "I believe I'm going to make it through this." But after a few months, when you're not getting call-backs from job interviews, anxiety sets in.

Now you're into another year of a personally slow economy and whatever dreams you had are dead and buried. You've been praying and attending church, but your situation is at a standstill. Let's be honest; there comes a point when you find it hard to talk to God because you think He's not listening.

Take note! What makes the problem even more difficult is not just the duration of the storm, but the heavy financial weights you are carrying. You are trying your best to hold onto everything you enjoyed before the tempest began—what you worked so hard for, and what is precious and dear to you.

31

Don't kick yourself for feeling the human response to disappointment. This is only natural.

There is nothing that can make us feel more burdened and stressed than money matters! Let's face it, it's the number one issue in our society. This is because we live in a consumer culture where glamour and fame is what millions are seeking.

The folly of chasing wealth or "things" causes us to have a "keeping up with the Joneses mentality" that, in turn, creates massive amounts of deficit spending, which is money we don't have.

When debt piles up the size of Mount Kilimanjaro, all hope seems lost. Then, when we downsize (with no savings to survive on because we spent it all searching for significance) despair sets it. So, trust me, I understand the struggle you might be in and want to share a secret to help you escape. It sounds simple, but it is wealth wisdom of both ancient and modern days. Here is the principle: **Sometimes you must let go of certain things for the short term in order to survive the financial storm you are in, so that you can live to fight and prosper another day!**

Holding on to a lifestyle that keeps you in the cycle of poverty and prevents you from entering the cycle of wealth is financial and maybe emotional suicide!

You must become comfortable with lightening your load so the stress and pressure can be removed from your heart and allow your soul to be restored.

Again, there is no storm like a financial storm, but before you throw up your hands in despair and cry, "I can see absolutely no way out," let me show the application of this principle through a storm in which Paul the Apostle found himself.

THE RIOT

After Paul had made several missionary journeys, the Lord instructed him to return to Jerusalem. While there, he felt led to visit the Temple and testify to the Jews about Christ the Messiah.

This didn't go over too well, to say the least. The Jewish high priest, Ananias, commanded the Roman centurions, who were in control of Judea and Jerusalem at the time, to arrest Paul.

However, Paul told a centurion, "You shouldn't be treating me like this because I'm a citizen of Rome." The officer responded, "Well, I am too, but I bought my citizenship." Paul exclaimed, "Not me. I was born a Roman citizen. You're supposed to be on my side!"

The centurion grew extremely nervous and took Paul to Felix, the governor. Felix agreed to hear Paul's case, and the apostle began his defense by telling of his experience with Jesus on the road to Damascus, and how his life had been radically transformed. The governor concluded, "Your accusers must have a chance to come before you."

So Felix invited the high priest and others to the prison quarters and asked, "What is your accusation against this man?"

Immediately, Paul entered into a conversation with them, saying, "There are both Pharisees and Sadducees here and I am a Pharisee. The only difference between us is that we (Pharisees) believe in angels—and that there is life after death. We believe in resurrection and the Sadducees don't."

Paul went on to explain that when he spoke of Jesus, he was talking about One who came back from the dead.

The high priest didn't buy into what Paul was saying, and kept up the pressure. So, Felix, not knowing what to do, agreed to hold Paul in jail, awaiting further counsel on the matter.

THE TRIBUNAL

After two long years, a new Roman governor named Festus took rule. A few days later, he heard of this "rabble-rouser" named Paul who remained isolated in prison. There were still many cases brought against Paul, mainly for the charge that he testified of Jesus.

After Festus heard the case, he too had no idea how to proceed. Then King Agrippa came to visit governor Festus, who told him, "I want you to hear what this man Paul has to say for himself. I can't find anything wrong with him—yet the locals want me to have him killed."

A major tribunal was ordered, with the king, the governor, the high priest, and a large crowd in attendance. Paul knew a storm was brewing, but he used the occasion to share his testimony and boldly proclaim Jesus Christ as the Son of God.

The apostle was convincing, but they were still calling for his head. The local authorities begged Festus and Agrippa, "Release him to us that we might kill him for what he says."

The officials responded, "No, we can't do what you ask, because he is a Roman citizen. We'll have to find another way around this situation."

Paul, knowing the law and his rights as a citizen, stood up and declared, "Wait a minute. Don't hand me over to these men. Send me to Rome, because under Roman law, every citizen can make an appeal to a jury of their peers and to the emperor himself. I'm a Roman citizen. I demand to see Caesar Augustus. Under the law of the land, you cannot deny me this right."

Soon the word was out in Jerusalem that if Paul was ever transported, he would be killed.

Under the darkness of night, surrounded by armed guards, Festus hustled Paul off to a boat headed for Rome—with other prisoners.

IS THE TIMING RIGHT?

Notice that although Paul's personal situation was very difficult in Jerusalem, **he requested to go to Rome.** Even though there were rumors that the locals were going to kill him, it would have been quite an international incident to have done so, spilling Roman blood.

Here's the point: There are many times we make decisions to get out of one storm, only to land in an even bigger tempest—as we will see in Paul's case.

Perhaps the apostle sailed in the wrong season, and he paid a high price for it. While we may argue that it was God's will for him to go to Rome, he didn't have to travel when he did and face the storm that almost killed him in the process of trying to do God's will..

We too must avoid moving in the wrong season—especially financial. In regard to wealth building, we must develop "patient money" that can bide its time, waiting to be spent later. For example, it is always the wrong season to overspend on housing, cars, clothing, or furniture.

As Paul and the other prisoners began their journey, the winds were gently catching the sails. They crossed the Mediterranean, passing Turkey and Greece, but between the islands of Cypress and Crete, the seas became choppy. Things then grew from bad to worse.

Perhaps, like you and me, Paul had an inkling that he was on a sinking ship. This is similar to the person who finds themselves behind on a car payment or two, and takes out a cash advance on a credit card to catch up. This can lead to even more dangerous waters.

Paul told the Roman centurion who was in charge of the boat, "There's land over there. I think we should head for shore as soon as possible."

There comes a time when we know that we have probably made a poor decision about getting out of a bad situation and we just need to stop and find land. Paul's call for the shore is perhaps the first indication that he knew he was headed for deeper trouble. Unfortunately, in his case, he was on a boat with a stubborn captain. It can be hard to survive storms, or at least find rest from them, when we are traveling with individuals who would rather go down with the ship! There are marriages in financial ruin because one spouse decides maintaining the illusion of a lifestyle is more important than the reality of a financial storm.

The man replied to Paul, "No. We're not going to dock now, because winter is coming. We need to reach a bigger port. If we don't, we won't be able to survive or make it through the months ahead." Undeterred, Paul continued, "Guys, I don't have a good feeling about this."

We, too, have likely had thoughts that our decisions were leading to our demise and a little voice whispered, "Perhaps this is not a good idea."

Usually, when our soul becomes heavy it means we

are on the wrong track. So whatever choices or behaviors have lead us to this point must be altered because if we stay on this train, the tracks could run off a cliff!

The commander, not wanting to take orders from a prisoner and thinking he knew better, ordered, "Let's keep sailing on."

Before long, however, *"a tempestuous head wind arose, called Euroclydon"* (Acts 27:14). In the U.S. we'd refer to it as a "Nor'easter."

Paul found himself in a named storm because he choose to go to Rome. Therefore, he had to accept that this was *his* predicament.

Are you in a financial whirlwind? Here is a simple way to tell:

- Do you have more garage doors than cars?
- Are you late on a mortgage or rent payment for a home that has a game room? Media room? Extra bedroom?
- Are you wearing your wealth on your back— luxury watches, clothing, shoes, and bags?
- Do you have an empty bank account but you have seen all of the latest movies, cable specials, and you dine out regularly?

This list is not exhaustive, but you get the point. If you have examined the above and come to the conclusion that you are in your named storm, don't lose hope. Paul shows us wisdom and a wealth secret that we can apply to every area of life.

How did the apostle land in this mess on the high seas? His storm may have been caused by impatience.

When we look back at the entire episode, we find that on the first night Paul was taken to prison after teaching in the Temple, the Bible records: *"The Lord stood beside Paul and said, 'Don't worry. Just as you have told others about Me in Jerusalem, you must also tell about Me in Rome"* (Acts 23:11).

The Lord didn't mention anything about a storm or a shipwreck—just that he was to give testimony in Rome.

However, Paul rushed the timetable. When he was in jail, frustrated and accused of being a liar and a heretic, he said, *"If I am an offender, or have committed anything deserving of death, I do not object to dying; but if there is nothing in these things of which these men accuse me, no one can deliver me to them. I appeal to Caesar"* (Acts 25:11).

The moment he uttered those words, everything changed. The Romans were obligated to send him immediately to Rome.

The Lord told Paul He wanted him to testify before Caesar, but didn't mention "when" or "now is the season." That was the apostle's doing, by saying he wanted to leave immediately.

Maybe Paul's impatience got the best of him, just like it did when he persecuted the Christians prior to coming to Jesus and denying the youthful Mark the privilege of accompanying him on a later missionary journey.

If Festus and Agrippa had waited until after winter to send their prisoner to Rome, there would have likely been no storm. **So Paul's predicament was the result of his impatience with the process.** He forgot that Isaiah had written, *"Those who wait on the Lord shall renew their strength"* (Isaiah 40:31). But Paul felt he couldn't wait any longer. Perhaps prison life was getting too tough.

There are times when we were trying to do the right thing, but our impulsive nature led us into a storm. We didn't *mean* to get saddled with debt, but we wanted everything now, not later.

You may receive a word from the Lord, but is it the right season for you to act? If you move in haste, that's not the time to start blaming God, saying, "How could You allow this to happen to me? How could You let me get into this storm? I was doing what I believe You told me to do."

Paul was given the correct assignment, but it wasn't the right season to sail.

DON'T BE THE CAUSE OF YOUR STORM

Before using the same remedy for every circumstance, make sure you know what type of storm you are in. For example, one trial may be self-inflicted, while another is meant to build your faith.

Have you ever heard of Jonah—the man sung about in Sunday School, who was thrown overboard and found himself in the belly of a whale? Well, Jonah's storm was because of his own rebellion. He was trying to run from God. That's a far cry from Paul, who was trying to obey the Lord, yet grew inpatient in the process.

So there are certain trials we face because we fail to listen to what God is telling us. Jonah was told to preach to the people of Nineveh; instead, he hopped on a ship headed for Tarshish.

As long as Jonah was a passenger on the boat, there was going to be big time trouble—because *he* was the problem. It wasn't until they agreed to throw Jonah overboard that the seas calmed. In other words, there are some situations, even financial, that won't be solved until you stop being their cause.

Jonah blamed the people of Nineveh for his problems and could not see until much later that it was his decision-making that created his own crisis. Never blame others for your financial storm; otherwise your lack of accountability could cause you to remain outside the cycle of wealth.

If you feel like you are in debt solely because banks took advantage of people with the mortgages they offered, or the company cut you unfairly, you might just miss the real issue. What about the overflow of goods that have accumulated in the closet, in the garage, and on the shelves that are now depreciated in value, wasted investments—and are no longer necessary?

In the end, while you might not be able to control the economy or your employer, you can do your part to not create the chaos that is the result of overspending and poor habits of saving.

DIVINE STORMS VS YOUR STORMS

A second type of storm is one designed to build your faith.

Once, at the Sea of Galilee, *"Jesus made His disciples get into the boat and go before Him to the other side"* while He stayed behind to pray (Matthew 14:21-22). In the middle of the night, a violent storm arose and Jesus walked on the water out to the vessel. The disciples were frightened, thinking they had seen a ghost, so Peter cried out, *"Lord, if it is You, command me to come to You on the water"* (verse 28).

The Bible records that Peter stepped out of the boat and tried to walk toward Jesus, but when he turned his eyes away from the Master and began to focus on the wind and waves, he started to sink. *"Immediately Jesus stretched out His hand and caught him, and said to him, 'O you of little faith, why did you doubt?'"* (verse 31). Then the wind ceased.

It's important to remember that Jesus *made* them get into the boat. There are some storms the Lord wants you to experience in order to fortify your faith and foster your development.

We can take great comfort that if the Lord brought us onto the water, He will get us across the water. God may have inspired you to stretch your faith, to move into a home, start a business, or expand a ministry. And even though things are tight and tough, He will be your miracle as long as you "consider not" the storm. These challenges are sent to build the character you need to handle greatness.

IF YOU WANT TO SURVIVE, GET RID OF SOME STUFF

On Paul's journey, the waves were swelling higher and the storm intensified, so as they passed the lee side of a small island called Calauda (about 20 miles south of Crete) they paused in the calmer waters and somehow managed to prepare a lifeboat to have on board. During this time, they were also able to wrap cables under the ship, hoping that would hold the vessel together.

Back at sea, as Paul describes it, *"Because we were exceedingly tempest-tossed, the next day they lightened the ship. On the third day, we threw the ship's tackle overboard and we did it with our own hands. Now when neither the sun nor the stars appeared for many days, and no small tempest beat on us, all hope that we would be saved was finally given up"* (Acts 27:18-20).

The wisdom applied here was to lighten the load. Yes, that's it!

When the "big one" hits, you're not going to weather the storm by trying to stubbornly hold onto everything you own. There will likely be some possessions you dearly love that you'll need to get rid of. If you try to keep sailing against winds that are stronger than you are, you will weaken your faith, your hope, and yourself. After all, if you had only listened to that "still small voice," you wouldn't even be in this situation.

I recently asked a businessman, "How's it going?" He replied, "Well, I'm just trying to keep this thing afloat."

This is exactly what millions are doing—transferring money from over here and using it over there. Juggling bills like a circus performer. "Let's see. If I take advantage of the 30-day grace period on bill X, I can use the money to pay bill Y on day 2." Those are the people who make a phone call on day 30, saying, "I'm sorry, but the check is in the mail"—knowing it takes a while for a check to clear.

The leaks in a person's "budget" boat can have many causes: remodeling a kitchen when they can't afford it; staying in a 5-star luxury hotel so they can impress their friends, eating lobster instead of linguini —and the list goes on and on and on.

You won't have to regret your actions, admitting, "I wish I hadn't done that," if you make the decision today to lighten the load that is weighing you down. It might mean losing a little of your standing in the community, or even some of those negative so-called friends who have been giving you bad advice.

Many see letting go as being a failure, and they are afraid to publically admit they've made a huge mistake. Or they feel they are letting God down, so they decide to fight it out. But if the storm is still there, you are the one who will have to take action—to toss overboard everything in your life that isn't absolutely necessary.

DECISION TIME

Perhaps you have found yourself in the clutches of a perfect financial storm and have reached the point where you've lost hope that your home, your job, or your business is going to survive. **Here is your life raft: It is okay to say goodbye to that which is a heavy weight. But time is of the essence and you must act quickly.**

The hurricane has hit you with full force; the waves are crashing in and you're about to go under drowning in debt. Now is the time to make some serious decisions. You've got to rid yourself of whatever has been dragging you down and holding your prosperity back. Do what the crew of the ill-fated vessel did when things got rough—they "lightened the ship" (verse 18)—and quickly began to throw things overboard.

If you keep clinging to the boat and losing hope, eventually, you will sink. And if you're drowning, it may even cause you to abandon God and blame Him for everything—your shipmates, the shoddy boat, even for the storm itself. It will be the fault of everything and everybody but you.

When your situation is spiraling out of control, don't let ego and pride keep you from downsizing for a while. You may have to drive a used car instead of a new one and cut up your credit cards until the sun begins to shine once more.

"QUITTING" IS NOT ALWAYS A BAD WORD

Popular author Seth Godin, in his book *The Dip*, says that we need to quit the wrong stuff to do the right stuff. It's as if Seth read the story about Paul the same way I did.

Seth argues that people often see letting go as something bad, but society is wrong to reach that conclusion. In fact, winners quit, and they do it quite often. I agree with Seth that successful individuals, and the most financially savvy, quit all the time.

For example, how many times have you read of famous business people who abandon a building project? They remain wealthy because they refused to lose all of their money on a bad investment. Yes, they began in good faith, but when it was obvious that it was a poor decision, they found a way to legally abandon the project and not go down with the ship.

Corporate America has prospered from throwing things overboard for eons; in fact, millions have lost their jobs because accountants decided to save on labor costs. And there are plenty of casualties because companies are trying to cut back on health care expenses.

Even on a governmental level, deficit spending can never sustain itself. In hard times they are forced to eliminate programs and lighten the load in order to return to fiscal health.

It makes no sense to keep a house or a car that costs too much, and credit cards that lead to personal stress and unhappiness, resulting in late night heart palpitations. Lighten your load!

If the Titanic is heading for an iceberg, I don't care how much you've paid for your ticket, it's time to bail!

Where God guides, He certainly provides and His possessions never become foreclosed, repossessed, or charged-off. This is why I implore you to stop holding on to what you think is so important and free your hands to grab hold of what God offers.

JESUS SAYS DOWNSIZING IS GAINING

If you are struggling with the concept of lightening your load, I want you to know that Jesus taught the principle that we must cut-back before we can have more in John 15. Christ said, *"I am the true vine, and My Father is the vinedresser. Every branch in Me that does not bear fruit He takes away; and every branch that bears fruit He prunes, that it may bear more fruit...If anyone does not abide in Me, he is cast out as a branch and is withered"* (verses 1-2, 6).

Let's examine this passage through the lens of wealth building wisdom. Christ describes three types of branches (as metaphors for servants) and the divine methods He uses to cause them to grow:

Branch #1: The Fruitful

Jesus says these faithful servants must be "pruned" in order to grow. This means they must be trimmed or cut back so that they can be more effective and productive.

At first glance, it seems unfair that good people must be demoted, yet, beneath the surface there is an incredible revelation: every time you trim a branch it grows back stronger and produces more than it did before. Even if you are doing okay, perhaps you could do better. There's still time to cut back your budget so that you can move from riches to wealth.

Branch #2: The Fruitless

The Lord declares that the fruitless must be repositioned to "abide in Me" so that they can grow. This means that they must move into another place or position to be more productive. These branches are not dead; they are just not in the right place.

The key is that they still have the ability to produce. Perhaps the branch is fruitless because it is being "blocked" by another branch, or maybe it is not getting enough water to build strength. Whatever the reason, this kind of servant must relocate to a more effective place to prosper.

Could God be trying to reposition you to another part of the country where jobs are in abundance, but you are being held back by your unwillingness to let go of the home where you live and the possessions you have?

Branch #3: The Withered

The major difference between the withered and the fruitless is that *the withered no longer have the ability to produce.*

No matter how hard you try to work with a withered branch, it won't thrive because its time has past. Jesus says we must move on from these branches and cast them aside.

In applying Jesus' teaching to our personal finances, do the branches represent your career or material possessions? Are they being fruitful, fruitless, or are they withering?"

Here is a simple truth: **Jesus says growth comes from cutting back.** This can be applied to everything —not just sanctification and spiritual maturity.

So rather than asking yourself if you are ready to let go, ask, "Do I *want* to grow?" If the answer is yes, then you must be willing to have your financial life "pruned" or "repositioned" so you will not waste away.

Do not let the enemy convince you to become one of the castaways.

The new lifestyle that God has planned for you may not be what you want today, but it will be where you can prosper for the future.

Let's get specific.

1. Perhaps you need to move to a smaller home or apartment. Yes, short-sell if you have to. If you are in dire straights, then foreclose. Your rebound may take time, but with better decisions tomorrow, you will be credit-worthy again.
2. Hand in the keys to your expensive automobile. Get a cheaper, more practical vehicle.
3. You may need to sell your business? If it is not profitable, seek the counsel of a lawyer and accountant to find out the best way to close it down.
4. Throwing things overboard also applies to toxic relationships, including ending a bad business partnership. However, this does *not* include marriage, or throwing away your spouse!

5. Cut up every credit card and operate on cash.
6. Sell luxury items and use the money to pay off credit card debt. Every time you see that big bill, your stress level rises and there is nothing that a material possession can do to lower your heart rate or cause you to sleep better at night.

I counseled a business owner who had over-expanded his operations to several states and multiple locations during the good times. The big recession hit and business tanked. In fact, his company was knee deep in debt from financing equipment and opening new stores.

With a mortgage to pay and college tuition to meet for his children, I told him, "Let this business go or your life will not grow."

It was tough, embarrassing, and painful. But after much legal and accounting counsel, the company was dissolved and the debt was resolved with the banks. It did not take long for this owner to get a fresh start. In fact, his recent years have been the best ever. Fewer locations and employees, less equipment; decreased stress but increased profit; better health, spending more time with his family, and being able to serve his local church.

This could be your story.

It's Time For A Financial Fast

The effects of American consumerism have trickled into every aspect of our lives. We've been self-consumed, self-indulgent, materialistic, and wasteful, and now our country, environment, livelihood, and even our children our suffering from it. Even in the most desperate of times, our culture is flooded with temporal wants and desires. Advertisers swoop down like vultures to tempt us with slanted images of the good life, wanting us to buy every piece of junk they advertize on television. Marketing executives target some of the most disadvantaged communities in our nation, enticing citizens to spend more on non-durable goods (in which there is more profit) than commodities. The marketers succeed because we have lost our interest in sacrificing today for a better tomorrow.

In my home, we periodically conduct what I call "financial fasts"—seasons where we downsize, cut back, spend less, sell items, etc. It reminds all of us that the good life requires sacrifice at times that may include our comforts.

In 2000, we had just moved into a brand new 4,000 sq. ft. home in the suburbs. I was at the top of my game in the corporate world, was making good money, and had a Jaguar to park in the three-car garage. It was the perfect time to practice a financial fast. A new mortgage and grander lifestyle was a reason to cut back and tighten the purse strings. We cut off our cable, lowered our phone service, decreased our restaurant outings, limited our shopping, and, yes, got rid of the Jag. I sold it and bought a "very used" Cadillac CTS.

I'm sure some people thought we had bitten off more than we could chew. The reality was just the opposite; I was pruning to grow. I was earning plenty of money, our investments were doing well, and I had just received a promotion.

True wealth requires discipline and making necessary sacrifices to reach one's goals. We weren't concerned about the Joneses and only cared about the pursuit, where the journey would lead us.

Ironically, a year later, I was terminated from my big-time New York City brokerage firm. The financial impact didn't hit us hard because we had already been living below our means and we knew how to tighten our belts. From my termination to the opening up of my own insurance brokerage firm, my family didn't have to make any major lifestyle adjustments.

That season of financial sacrifice proved to be prophetic indeed. There is nothing like a fast to help us trim down the flesh. That's why I believe in going on a diet from debt accumulation, reckless recreational spending, and the like.

What about you? Do you need to sell a few beloved items in order to move to the next level?

You May Be Shipwrecked, But You're Not Sunk!

I hope you are being released to move toward prosperity by walking away from the material-chasing that has caused the worst financial storm of your life. We have plenty to learn from the journey of the Apostle Paul. In the midst of the tempest, he and his fellow prisoners threw everything overboard. But they still found themselves in the storm and it was hard to survive.

Trying to get your financial house in order so that you may prosper will not be easy, but I believe you are up to the task. The Bible tells us that the men aboard the ill-fated ship were able to fashion together a lifeboat (Acts 27:16-17).

I love the fact the Lord always makes a way for us, even in the roughest of situations. The storm raged and the boat fell apart, but they held on to the broken wood and made it to an island called Malta.

There are lifeboats ready to help you with your finances. There are countless credit card counseling agencies, mortgage foreclosure bureaus, and restructuring organizations that will guide you through the storm and get your feet on solid ground again.

Let me share more good news; there will always be another boat, just like there was for Paul (Acts 28:11). The Bible says it took a few months for another ship to come, but it did.

The reason Paul could announce to the men on the sinking ship, *"There will be no loss of life among you,"* was because God told him, *"you must be brought before Caesar; and indeed God has granted you all those who sail with you"* (Acts 27:22,24). Isn't that beautiful? Even though I suggest Paul moved in the wrong season, the Father's grace would not allow him to sink—His grace is sufficient.

The apostle was letting those on board know, "I will survive so I can continue to do what I am supposed to do. The ship doesn't matter."

Can you say the same thing? "God has a plan for my future. The house, the car, the clothes, and all these high-tech gadgets are not important."

Paul regained his hope because he heard from an angel *"of the God to whom I belong and whom I serve"* (verse 23).

Just because the skies are ominously black, remember Who you serve. It's not money, or material "things," but the Creator of the Universe. Throw everything overboard, but make sure you keep Jesus in your boat.

Paul was sailing on the high seas in a vessel filled with unbelievers—prisoners and Roman centurions. He was the only follower of Christ.

Today, you might be the only one in your family to hear from heaven. Those close to you may not know the Lord, and are complaining, "How are we going to get through this?"

Instead of listening to their discouragement, get alone and receive a word from God for your loved ones, and firmly hold onto hope!

While Paul may have found himself in trouble because he was impetuous, he knew who he was in Christ. He could declare:

- I am a new creature in Christ (2 Corinthians 5:17).
- I am God's workmanship (Ephesians 2:10).
- I am a joint-heir with Christ (Romans 8:17).
- I am the righteousness of God in Jesus Christ (2 Corinthians 5:21).
- I am more than a conqueror through Him who loves me (Romans 8:37).
- I am an ambassador for Christ (2 Corinthians 5:20).
- I am alive with Christ (Ephesians 2:5).

The financial storm may endure much longer than you imagined. The going may get tough, but hang in there. As the psalmist declared, *"I have been young, and now am old: yet I have not seen the righteous forsaken"* (Psalm 37:25).

Never be tempted to believe that the storm you are going through is the result of divine punishment. Examine how you got there, and remember that the Lord's plans don't change just because the weather does. Make a commitment to stay the course because He is going to work all things for your good—because He loves you.

Have faith that God will do what He has promised. Whether He says you will testify in Rome, or to your Uncle Ralph, just know that when your heavenly Father directs you, He will deliver you.

"A TIME TO THROW AWAY"

As we learned in chapter 1, God has designed the cycle of wealth with entrance ramps and exits. Living above our means is the quickest way to exit the cycle —or never find your way onto it in the first place. It may be time to cut your lifestyle way back.

We've all heard the phrase popular among health and fitness aficionados: "no pain, no gain." It suggests that we'll never achieve our goals for a new body if we don't put in the effort and endure the discomfort of pushing our muscles to their limit. The same can be said for hope and prosperity, or simply living your dream: *No pain, no gain.*

If you're one of those individuals afraid of "giving a little to get a little" to improve your finances, you might as well quit your wealth dream now. You'll never get there.

People who are fearful of fiscal sacrifice will never achieve abundance. If you can win with Jesus by losing your life, then you can succeed at wealth building by losing the mentality that leads from one small storm to a greater one.

Remember, you may be shipwrecked, but you're not sunk. Today, the Lord is telling you, there is *"a time to gain, and a time to lose; a time to keep, and a time to throw away"* (Ecclesiastes 3:6).

Don't avoid lightening your load when it is necessary. There will be another day, another blessing. The next boat is on its way!

Remember these wealth building secrets:

- Never blame others for your financial problems.
- Don't hesitate to lighten your debt load.
- Quitting is not always a bad word. Winners quit the wrong stuff to do the right stuff!
- Pruning material things from your life produces increase.
- Understand the true cause of your storm.
- Make sure you do things in the right season.
- Sometimes you have to lose short-term to gain long-term.
- You may be shipwrecked, but you're not sunk.
- Remember, there will always be another boat.

TAP INTO YOUR POWER TO GET WEALTH

EVERY PERSON IS CREATED WITH "THE ABILITY" TO BE AN ENTREPRENEUR

There's a verse in Scripture that has been quoted and misquoted more times than you could count. It's where Moses told the children of Israel that God would give them "power to get wealth."

Wow! Who wants to bypass that opportunity? So we lift up our hands and say, "Okay, Lord. Give it to me! I want that power! I want that wealth!"

Sorry to burst your bubble, but until you read the entire verse—and the passage leading up to it—you'll never receive what God has ordained.

Read slowly, so as not to miss one word: *"You shall remember the Lord your God, for it is He who gives you power to get wealth, that He may establish His covenant which He swore to your fathers, as it is this day"* (Deuteronomy 8:18).

There is a *reason* God gives you this power—and it's overlooked by those who only like to quote the first part of this verse. It is so *"He may establish His covenant."*

When I asked a Rabbi friend what this verse means to Israel, he drew the same conclusion that I did, adding, "God provides all types of goodness and we must thank Him. If not for expression of gratitude, we would lose sight of its source (see Deuteronomy 8: 11-12 and again 8:14). Then in verse 17, it speaks of man believing that he, not God, is responsible for all his success, at least that is how we see it," he concluded.

This means that Almighty God has tied Himself to our prosperity. He has joined the financing of the expansion of His earthly kingdom to our personal wealth building. One must stop to think, if God has done this, He must feel rather confident that we can create wealth and use it to effectuate His plans for the earth. It's clear that His covenant includes a provision for money.

What is that covenant? In Genesis 17, the Almighty told Abraham, *"I will make nations of you, and kings shall come from you. And I will establish My covenant between Me and you and your descendants after you*

in their generations, for an everlasting covenant"
(verses 6-7). In God's view, these words are set in stone. He
wants to make nations and kings for Himself. God's
plan demands financiers, like Abraham. Notice that
the Lord made Abraham wealthy and prospered him
before Isaac was born. If you search through Scripture
with a financial eye, you will also see that where God
guides, He always provides. After years of slavery, He
sent the children of Israel out of Egypt carrying with
them the wealth of the Egyptians.

The Lord's covenant is not finished or terminated;
it is everlasting, which means His plan for financing the
kingdom expansion must be ongoing today. Printing
Bibles, creating profitable Christian businesses, building churches, Christian websites, apps, making Christian movies, etc., are costly. They are all part of the
covenant for God to create a people, and each of
these requires our support and funds.

So the Lord has given us a power that we can use
to build personal kingdom wealth. The reason it is
personal is because we do it with the gifts and abilities
we have been given. It is also *kingdom*, because we
are *supposed* to use it to spread the message of Christ.
So think of it this way, by giving us a power to get
wealth for this purpose, the Almighty has united His
plans with us and is taking a big risk—trusting that we

will do the right thing with the wealth He has allowed us to create.

You're an Heir

In the New Testament, after the Day of Pentecost, when Peter was preaching at a location known as Solomon's Porch, he told the gathered crowd that the outpouring of the Spirit that was taking place had been promised through a divine contract with their ancestors—to both Jews and Gentiles: *"[God] said to Abraham, 'All nations on earth will be blessed because of someone from your family.' [He] sent His chosen Son to you first, because God wanted to bless you and make each one of you turn away from your sins."* (Acts 3:25-26 CEV).

Later, Paul the Apostle explained to believers, *"If you are Christ's then you are Abraham's seed, and heirs according to the promise"* (Galatians 3:29). Paul let them know the very same privileges of the covenant with Abraham extended beyond Israel to all Gentiles who come through Christ, and this includes the ability or power to create wealth, which is in operation for our benefit today; we simply have to tap into it and use it purposefully.

The Lord is not as concerned with you having wealth as He is with what you are going to do with it.

62

His desire is that you use your resources to build the kingdom—and the covenant He instituted.

Neither the world or our Creator needs another haughty, arrogant Christian to get rich and flaunt wealth in the face of the "faithless" and hopeless. **Instead, the world needs wealthy Christians with a heart for God, who will use their resources to solve the planet's problems in a manner that is pleasing to the Almighty.**

No one is excluded from the cycle of wealth, regardless of what situation they were born into. There is a secret yet to be revealed through the work of your mind or hands. When what is undisclosed is made known to the marketplace, you will reap the rewards of profit and be able to sow that profit into the covenant.

WHAT'S YOUR POWER?

I believe the power to acquire wealth speaks to the entrepreneur in all of us. I can say this confidently and without reservation, regardless of someone's economic or educational background.

The recent successes of Micro-Business programs in Third World countries prove that even poor people with little education can make money using their hands and minds. With as little as $1,000 in funding from the World Bank, the situations of many have improved substantially.

God has given you the ability to make money from a skill, work ethic, ability, or idea that you have. In fact, the whole Bible is full of enterprises, start-ups, and ventures.

Since the ancient world did not have corporations, this means that everyone, from Adam to the leaders of the early New Testament church and afterwards, made and sold something to gain wealth—*and they did not have a string of degrees after their names!*

The Bible never speaks of Abraham's education, yet we know that he was a wealthy man. The same is true of Isaac, Joseph, David, and Solomon. In New Testament days, we read of individuals such as Joseph of Arimathea and Lydia who used their riches for God's work, but nothing is written of their education.

Wealth is within us, waiting to be unlocked.

The book *Start-Up Nation*, chronicles how the Jewish people have been able to survive and thrive by being entrepreneurial and making or selling ideas and products. It documents the fact that today Israel is literally a nation of successful startups. They are operating in the power to acquire wealth through the principles the Bible reveals.

The power for wealth is an ability or idea the Creator places within us at birth. We are endowed with the might and strength to see that promise fulfilled.

While it's true that some people identify how they can make money sooner than others, the potential for entrepreneurship lies in each of us. And it can be achieved in thousands of different ways.

My father had the power and natural ability to fix cars. His love for automobiles started when he was young. He'd find old parts and actually build a vehicle that would run. This talent led him to Detroit, where he worked at the Ford Motor Company, learning to develop his skills even further. Then he moved to New Jersey and dad opened his own auto garage.

However, my father's power wasn't mine. Oh, my brother and I tinkered around his shop, but we were just playing in the grease!

My skills were different. I was curious as to how things worked. So I learned to make robots. I couldn't fix a car, but I could make a box walk! That interest led me down a corporate track, and to ultimately opening my own business.

Each of my brothers and sisters developed their individual power to attain wealth through their life experiences. For example, one of my sisters had some trials and tribulations with her health when she was young. This did not defeat her; instead, it led her to medical school and becoming a doctor.

JOSEPH IS THE MODEL FOR
UNLOCKING YOUR WEALTH POWER

I believe the power to get wealth refers to every human's ability to do something entrepreneurial. It speaks to the God-given abilities we have that we can use for industry.

An amazing Old Testament story proves the point.

In chapter 1, we saw how Abraham left a blessing that was inherited by his son Jacob. Unfortunately, Jacob temporarily exited the cycle of wealth when he sided with his older sons and rebuked his younger son, Joseph, for sharing a prophetic vision stating that the family was going to lose their wealth and eventually bow to him. Jacob asked Joseph, *"Shall your mother and I and your brothers indeed come to bow down to the earth before you?"* (Genesis 37:10).

Joseph's brothers became so consumed with envy, that they threw him into a pit, rubbed blood on his robe, and took the stained garment back to their father, telling him that an animal had killed their brother. In truth, the brothers sold Joseph into slavery to a passing band of merchants.

He was taken to Egypt and bought by one of Pharaoh's administrators. But because of a false accusation, Joseph wound up languishing in prison.

The pit, was bad enough, but prison was even worse. However, he was not forgotten. Even in that terrible situation, God had a plan for Joseph's future.

As a slave, Joseph stood out because of his excellent work ethic and extraordinary skill, which landed him his first job in Potiphar's house. Joseph refused to let the stigma and baggage of slavery affect his vision from God and he continued to press forward. As you know, he was "hit on" by the wife of his boss who flirted with him at a company party.

Since Joseph's policy was to remain honorable before God in all things, he rebuffed her advances. Despite this, he was falsely accused and thrown into prison.

Now Joseph had an official record as a criminal, which would no doubt make it tough for him to get a job in the future. Yet, in spite of this setback, Joseph never gave up on his vision or hope of success. At this point he had lost his family, his job, and had the emotional baggage of slavery playing on his psyche during his lonely hours of incarceration.

DEMONSTRATE YOUR POWER

Joseph was left with nothing but an ability to interpret dreams and wisdom for financial planning. All he needed was an opportunity to demonstrate His gift—and God gave it to him. In prison, he correctly interpreted the dreams of two inmates—a butler and a baker. Then, two years later, when Pharaoh had a dream that no one could explain, the butler, who had been freed, told Pharaoh about Joseph's unique gift.

The king was so impressed with Joseph's abilities that he was hired on the spot. In spite of being racially and ethnically different, poor, basically uneducated (by Egyptian standards), emotionally scarred by bearing the title of slave, plus having a criminal record, his talent earned him a job. It wasn't just any assignment, Joseph became the chief administrator of Egypt and private counsel to Pharaoh.

This is the first historical record we have of the job description of an executive coach and business consultant—helping a prominent leader with insights into the marketplace.

One of the sub-plots of this story is that it's a good idea to "show your stuff"—as Joseph did to the butler in prison regarding the fact he could interpret dreams. You never know how you can be blessed through a demonstration.

It also shows how we can use our abilities for future opportunities—even if we don't have a perfect record. This should be encouraging news to any person behind bars, knowing that if he was good at cutting grass before being locked up, he can start his own landscaping business after release!

As a result of interpreting the king's dream, Joseph made the first business 'pitch' we know of. He created a plan to buy wheat during the good years at depressed prices, then sell it for a profit in lean years. When you read the story, Joseph had his dream when he was just 17 years old, living in his father's house in Israel. It involved sheaves of wheat. He told his brothers, *"My sheaf arose and also stood upright; and indeed your sheaves stood all around and bowed down to my sheaf"* (Genesis 37:7).

Now, in Egypt, Joseph had nothing but a God-given dream that wheat would be under his control. He didn't have the finances to make this happen. But just like the high tech entrepreneurs of today, who pitch venture capitalists or angel investors to fund a vision, Joseph moved forward.

His plan was to corner the market on wheat, so he sold Pharaoh on an idea for creating an ancient industrial revolution that would lead to mutual prosperity. His plan would require Pharaoh to fund the building of huge silos to store grain that he would buy from both local and foreign markets. Those were the warehouses. In other words, **he had the dream, but he used "other people's money" to finance it.**

Then he advertized and marketed his new business to everyone, like putting out lawn signs that read, "Will Buy Grain for Cash."

Understand How
the Marketplace Works

Of course, when times are good people love cash. The problem is that many don't prepare for the "down times"—that sustain them through a harsh winter or a severe drought. So when the financial storms arise, they have consumed everything they needed to survive. In boom times people have a tendency to buy expensive cars, big houses, brand name clothing, you name it.

In the recent recession, we saw middle and upper middle class men and women join the working poor; in part because they lived for the day with no consideration of tomorrow.

Joseph knew that things were going to change so he played the market, basically creating the rule we still use today: buy low and sell high. He understood what many have failed to learn:

- The time to buy the expensive house is after it has been foreclosed on for a fraction of its original value.
- The time to buy that luxury car is after it's been repossessed from the person who can no longer afford the payments.

- The time to buy a designer handbag is from the second hand store that paid cash to the woman who needed to pay her rent.

This is how the rich keep getting richer. They make their moves when most people are suffering, then sit back and watch others buy their invested assets at inflated prices during boom times. The wealthy know they will recover what they spent as soon as the tide turns, and like a vulture waiting for the castaway to die in the desert, they patiently maneuver markets to buy at the bottom and sell at the top. The poor do just the opposite—which is a recipe for financial ruin.

GOD WILL PLACE YOU IN A POSITION TO PROSPER

During seven years of plenty (as detailed in Pharaoh's dream) Joseph filled the warehouses to the brim. Then came the seven-year famine.

Joseph began to implement the second phase of his plan, which was to open retail grocery stores to sell the people back what he had bought at lower prices. He created a chain of stores in the region and he and Pharaoh became extremely wealthy.

Both Egypt's aristocracy and foreigners had to come

to Joseph's grocery stores to buy his wheat; otherwise they would starve in the famine. His was the only game in town and he had cornered the market. Since there was no regulatory body controlling the fair market value, the price for grain was whatever Joseph said it was.

While I fully understand the Christological and expositional themes of Joseph—family, faith, obedience, and trusting in God—let me focus on a clear exegetical theme that is often overlooked or poorly treated: God plans for His people to prosper—and is constantly placing us in a position to do so. You can see the divine hand of God on Joseph's wealth building plan.

TRUE WEALTH STARTS WITH AN IDEA

Whatever wealth is, this story shows that it does not begin with money, but with an idea. For instance, Mark Zuckerberg didn't have any financial resources when he started Facebook—just a concept. But the money found him and he's a billionaire today.

When the Bible speaks of the power to gain wealth (Deuteronomy 8:18), it is referring to skills and abilities that God gives to us to manifest the ideas we have. The biblical way to abundance that has prospered both believers and unbelievers alike, is to have an inspiration, raise capital, and create profits for reinvestment into more ideas. This is the part many Christians fail to realize when they find themselves stuck on empty and exhausted from naming, claiming, and sowing.

I believe Joseph gives us a picture of what, centuries later, John envisioned for the church: *"Beloved, I pray that you may prosper in all things and be in health, even as your soul prospers"* (3 John 1:2).

To John, the Jewish context for prosperity would have been that which is released from personal initiative and the work of one's hands, not relying on the government or the church to create income for you.

After all, how could John expect these outside entities to produce wealth when the Roman government did everything it could to overtax the Jews and harass their ventures. Moreover, the church was poorly funded in the first century. In fact, the Apostle Paul bluntly told the believers in Thessalonica, *"If anyone will not work, neither shall he eat"* (2 Thessalonians 3:10).

In Bible times, prosperity was tied to industry—a fundamental understanding we are missing in today's society.

GOD MEANT IT FOR GOOD

Remember, Joseph's father, Jacob, was born into abundance, but because of disobedience, the entire family found themselves outside of God's cycle of wealth. The famine they experienced was so devastating that Jacob had to send his sons to Egypt to buy enough grain just to stay alive.

If you know the story, the brothers had to bend their knees before the governor of Egypt and beg for supplies. They had no idea it was Joseph they were bowing to—and that the dream he had as a teenager was being played out before their very eyes.

Finally, Joseph revealed himself to his astounded siblings, saying:

I am Joseph your brother, whom you sold into Egypt. But now, do not therefore be grieved or angry with yourselves because you sold me here...God sent me before you to preserve a posterity for you in the earth, and to save your lives by a great deliverance. So now it was not you who sent me here, but God; and He has made me a father to Pharaoh, and lord of all his house, and a ruler throughout all the land of Egypt (Genesis 45:4-5, 7-8).

The word *posterity* in the passage above means an *estate*. Joseph was telling them, "God graciously blessed me so that the family name would not continue in a cycle of poverty. It is our right to be born with an inheritance. If God had not taken me out of that pit and poured favor into my life; if I hadn't worked hard in Egypt to get recognized, I would not be in this position to bless you and save our estate. This is why God preserved me to bring our family back into the cycle of wealth and leave an inheritance for future generations."

I pray this story hits home. Are you taking ownership of the cycle of wealth for your family? Are you willing to do whatever it takes to produce gain for the next generation?

WEALTH BUILDING IS NOT 9 TO 5, BUT 5 TO 9

Perhaps you can now say, "Yes, I believe that I have the ability to create something because God needs me to prosper."

Allow me to help you understand how true wealth is created. Most are unaware that roughly 80 percent of America's millionaires are first-generation rich.[1] This means that the majority of new wealth in this country is coming from entrepreneurs—people who make their money themselves. These are ordinary men and women like you and me who started in 9-to-5 jobs, many working hard and only receiving income from a "J-O-B." That made them, in the words of investor and author Farrah Gray, "Just Over Broke."[2]

Business ownership has become a major source of wealth for the nouveau riche. Everyday folks who took their ideas and had the courage and will to turn them into self-owned businesses, building them from scratch. Entrepreneurial spirit has always fueled this country. According to the authors of the bestseller book, *The Millionaire Next Door*, chances are that if you meet a millionaire, he or she probably owns a business.[3] This is a testimony to our human ability or power to create wealth.

Small businesses employ approximately 55 percent of the workforce.[4] They account for the majority of everyday jobs in almost every industry—construction, retail, professional, scientific, software and technology, personal services, healthcare, social assistance, hospitality, food service, administrative support, ministries, etc.

These are the occupations we grew up idolizing. The average person believes that the large multinational corporations such as Microsoft, UPS, and Walmart employ the majority of American workers, but they do not. The typical American works for small business owners who decided one day that working 9-to-5 was not profitable enough, that they could have greater earning potential and growth if they worked for themselves. So they began building their own dreams and wealth. It turned into a full-time endeavor and they eventually employed others.

My friend, Jim, once told me that the entrepreneurial experience matches what he once heard from his immigrant grandparents: "Saved up enough money to buy a shovel. Made a few dollars digging holes, then bought a wheelbarrow. Made money digging bigger holes, and bought an old truck. Dug a lot of big holes, then I hired guys to dig holes with me."

This may sound humorous, but it is based on truth.

The majority of Americans will never build wealth and acquire financial freedom solely clocking in for somebody else on a 9-to-5 basis. You must also know what it means to start at 5 and work to 9! When you invest this much time and energy, you will quickly discover what you're capable of doing. You will soon learn if you have what it takes to be successful and build a lucrative business.

WEALTH IS WITHIN YOUR REACH

So many focus on the risk and failure of starting a

new venture that they never have the faith to take the first leap to create more opportunity and wealth for themselves. Remember, God blessed all human beings, with the ability to *"be fruitful and multiply"* (Genesis 1:28).

Since God is the Creator of the universe and we are made in His image and likeness, we should not be hesitant or afraid to either show or share our ideas with the world.

Have you ever brainstormed and had a such brilliant idea that you wanted to turn it into a business or a service you could offer? Well, this is not pie in the sky! You can spend your time doing just that. I'm not advising you to quit your job tomorrow—since working for others provides valuable experience needed to be a successful business owner. It's important to build skill sets and it takes a wide variety of knowledge to run a company. So treat working for others as a rite of passage.

The book mentioned earlier, *The Millionaire Next Door*, provided a new portrait of what real American millionaires look like. It demystified the idea of the wealthy "elite," and let the average person know that wealth was within the reach of any American. You, or your child, could be the up-and-coming millionaire next door.

Most of the super-successful people the authors

interviewed started building their 5-to-9 until it became their 9-to-5. Like many of us, they simply launched businesses to have a better life, financial freedom, and control over their own destiny. They came from humble beginnings and faced different types of challenges, yet they believed in this great country and the opportunity it continues to provide every one of its citizens for the pursuit of happiness. They each had a vision and the will and determination to see their dream through until it was a reality. They value education, have a solid work ethic, and put in far more hours than they ever did on someone else's payroll. Most important, they never lost faith.

WEALTH BUILDING BEGINS BY CREATING MULTIPLE INCOME STREAMS

Like it or not, you need money to gain access to just about everything in America: healthcare, housing, nutrition, education, even your own funeral.

We live in a consumer-based economy, so we need more than our regular jobs to forge ahead. How far can you get on a yearly zero to 3 percent annual raise—if that? So if you want to build wealth, it's imperative to create more than one income stream.

Starting a part-time business affords you the opportunity to increase your earning power.

Many men and women don't know what they're worth. They've never calculated the dollar value of their skills, gifts, and talents in the marketplace. If they do, their assessment may be based on emotions and insecurities rather than hard facts.

The first step to wealth creation is to adequately assess your abilities. Know what you can do, what you have to offer and, especially, what someone is willing to pay for your skills or services.

In launching a new enterprise, it's vital that you determine when to begin. Any excuse regarding the wrong time, i.e. the kids are too small, lack of money, things are too hectic at work, you're too old, etc., are irrelevant. Remember, the Bible says this wealth creating power is within you and it is part of God's covenant plan for you to reach your maximum potential.

You might be tempted to look at the economy, and complain that we're barely out of a recession, many are still facing an uncomfortably high unemployment rate, and banks and investors are tight-pursed when it comes to backing budding enterprises. Maybe your job was one of the 7.4 million plus cut from payrolls since the onset of the recession in December, 2007.[5]

You may be out of work and fearful of your financial well-being, so you're hitting the pavement on the hunt for a secure job, one with a steady paycheck, structure, and health insurance. Those fears are normal in uncertain times, but they should not stop you from considering entrepreneurship.

According to the U.S. Bureau of Labor Statistics, there were more than 9 million self-employed workers in 2008.[6] For many, this was a blessing in disguise. It jump-started countless men and women to find the gusto to launch their business ideas into a viable source of income. It's still happening. There are those who feel that it's just as risky finding employment in such an unsteady economic climate with no end in sight for job loss as it is starting a new venture. The fact is, millions of the newly unemployed are highly qualified and a good chunk of them have received their pink slips from companies that were once the leaders in their industry. They are waking up to the realization that their past experience gave them what it takes to go into business for themselves. They are taking the plunge.

WEALTH BUILDING MAY BE YOUR CHURCH WORK

In the Christian world, we often call serving, "church work." I hope you realize that becoming involved in your local church and serving with excellence may be the best way to identify and unlock your power to succeed. It makes sense.

Perhaps this is what Jesus was hinting at when He told us to *seek the kingdom first and everything else we need would be added* (Matthew 6:33).

Our service or apprenticeship does not need to be confined to church but can extend to interning with local non-profits and business owners. Remember, Lot would have never been wealthy without learning some skills from Abraham and working in his ministry.

Find an outreach of the church or business you think will help you attain your goal and offer to serve there, even if it's part-time or as an unpaid intern. Learn valuable insights from someone who is already doing it—a person who has some ministry excellence or entrepreneurial capital in play. Work for them. Study them. Pay attention to the different aspects of the organization and the skill sets needed. How do they manage? What are their inefficiencies? What are they good at? How do they gain the attention of those they serve, whether church members, customers, or patrons? How do they get materials or manufacture them? How do they promote their services? Learn— and learn some more.

Success rarely happens overnight. Many achievers spent years and years gaining knowledge, and even failing, before they started their ventures, let alone reaping the benefits.

In the business world, watching entrepreneurs run their companies and getting involved is a valuable tool of opportunity. You can learn management, financial planning, accounting, human resources, sales, and marketing skills. In addition, at church, you can get involved in marketing (evangelism), customer service (congregational care), custodial services, valet and special events (ushering and parking), assimilation (recruiting), public speaking (teaching, preaching, small groups), and so much more.

It is my prayer that you will see the endless potential at your fingertips. Your good service can turn into a class called "Entrepreneur 101."

LITA'S STORY

I know of a woman I'll call Lita. She was one of the most joyful children's ministry workers I've ever known. Interestingly, if you took inventory of her education and experience, one might say that she would have very few prospects on the job market. She has neither a college education nor a high school diploma. She lacks any corporate work experience or access to unlimited wealth from her family. She is blue collar all the way, but she is also a business owner.

Lita turned her love of working in children's ministry to offering babysitting services, expanding it into a lucrative home child-care business. She enjoyes taking care of kids and has been doing it for quite some time. It started out with babysitting a child or two in her home, then working for several parents in the neighborhood. Eventually, it blossomed into a full-fledged daycare center. She is now able to provide for herself using a talent she loves.

Lita's story shows how anybody can turn their life around if they have the will.

Never underestimate yourself. You have worth that people will pay for. Even more, the Lord wants you to succeed so you will sow into the kingdom.

We do not have to sit back and, with envy, watch others create new streams of income; we can do it ourselves. Take your hobbies, interests, and passions and cash in on them today. Love sports? Start a business for sports fans. Love food? Start a restaurant or a sandwich shop. Are you a proficient typist? Do you have excellent organizational and administrative skills? Why not start a company where you outsource yourself to small businesses that may not be able to afford a full-time assistant?

If you really enjoy cleaning and your house can pass the white glove test, perhaps you can start a cleaning or janitorial services company. You'll be surprised at what you can do if you put your mind to it.

Maybe you just like basketball. Why not launch a basketball camp for kids in your community for those who love the sport as much as you do?

Do you have a family recipe that has been passed down to you? Why not capitalize on it? Your product or service has to come from something that is *in* you. It's the only way you're going to have the passion you need to work those extra hours.

Parlay your skills into financial income. Millions of dollars are locked up in every human being and the only thing you need to do is start thinking about who you are, what you love to do, and what you're willing to accomplish. You can make it happen. But don't just run out there without much prayer and thought: count the cost.

WEALTH BUILDING IS EASIER WITH AN IMPARTATION FROM OTHERS

God gives the power to attain wealth in countless ways—including having it imparted from any person He wishes to use.

Just as Jesus learned to make furniture from His carpenter-father Joseph, you can learn to make or sell something from another person.

You may ask, "Does that mean that the gift God gives one individual can be transferred to another?"

85

Absolutely—but only if it is in the will of the Father.

Look at the life of the great prophet, Elijah. God used him to multiply the flour and oil of the poor woman of Zarephath (1 Kings 17:14), call fire down from heaven (1 Kings 18:38), strike the waters of Jordan with his mantle and they parted (2 Kings 2:8), plus more miracles.

When the day came that God was about to take Elijah to heaven in a whirlwind, his faithful servant, Elisha, cried out, *"Please let a double portion of your spirit be upon me"* (2 Kings 2:9).

When Elijah disappeared from sight, Elisha picked up the mantle that fell from the sky. Then he walked over to the river and struck the water with it—just as Elijah had. The same thing happened. According to Scripture, *"it was divided this way and that; and Elisha crossed over"* (verse 14).

Earlier, Elijah raised the son of the Zarephath widow from the dead (1 Kings 17:17-24). This amazing power was also given to Elisha. He, too, raised the son of a Shunammite woman from the sting of death (2 Kings 4:8-37).

This was not just a coincidence. The anointing was transferred by God from one prophet to the next. And the miracles *increased*. The Bible records eight miracles during the ministry of Elijah—and sixteen through Elisha. If that's not a double portion, I don't know what is!

There is an old saying: "Get under the spout where the glory comes out!" When you find a godly person with a gift from above—whether it be for healing, teaching, finances, or whatever, stay close to that individual and allow the same anointing to fall on you. What happened in the past is just prologue. What the Lord imparts to you can far supercede anything your mind can conceive. In God's realm, things progress from good, to better, to best.

WHO WILL BE YOUR MENTOR?

Find yourself a business mentor. If you can select one in your field, that would be ideal. The most important thing is to learn from a person who is successful and has already been through the growing pains of starting and operating an enterprise. This is your first form of leverage. According to Mark Hansen, author of the bestselling *Chicken Soup* series, "Your mentor knows the terrain, the challenges, the pitfalls. You mentor knows what to do. More important, your mentor knows what NOT to do."[7]

Find a well-respected, successful entrepreneur you admire. Maybe there's somebody in the company where you work, or your church—a person whom you believe can really help you. It could be an individual you have read about in the newspaper. Don't be intimidated or afraid to reach out to them. Write a letter and let them know that you are looking for a guiding hand.

I have received many such requests, and even though I am not able to help them all, I have developed a mentoring relationship with some.

Again, this is going to require your initiative and a desire to succeed. Don't sit back and feel that you're alone simply because you didn't reach out to those who had the potential to help. Insecurities can stop you from making a divine connection with a man or woman who could be instrumental in advancing your professional goals.

Entrepreneurial mentors can become like moms or dads. Perhaps we should call them "entrepreneurial parents" since they counsel and advice on what and what not to do. They can share unbiased information and steer you to the best banks or sources of funding. From them you can learn how to manage employees, market your products, build an influential board of directors, and they may even allow you to tap into their network.

Connecting with the right entrepreneurial parent will allow you to get the most out of your mentoring relationship. However, they must believe in your dream and agree that you can pull this off.

The worst thing you can do is to interact with someone who is pessimistic, unsupportive, or who is going to be overly critical, making you feel like there is no way in the world you can make your vision happen. A good entrepreneurial parent will motivate you, not tear you down. He or she should make themselves available and be willing to follow your progress. Make sure your mentor is a person of integrity who is full of energy, so that when you have doubts, they can lift your spirits with their strength.

It's vital that your mentor has a proven track record of success. It's widely known that the mentors of the world's most admired mentor, Warren Buffet, were Benjamin Graham, who many consider to be the dean of financial analysis, and Philip Fisher, called one of the greatest investors of all time. Buffet credits most of his success to these individuals. He once commented, "I am 15 percent Fischer and 85 percent Benjamin Graham."[8]

Find people who are respected in the community by their peers. From them you can glean wisdom and knowledge. They can impart the "entrepreneurial gene."

DEVELOP YOUR "ENTRPRENEURIAL GENE"

I had been encouraging a young friend of mine to

start his own business since 1992. His career trajectory was stellar and he boasted much success in corporate America. He was one of the brightest individuals I had ever met; inspiring, confident, had tremendous drive, and a unique ability to connect with people.

I felt that there was something bigger in store for him, and that his talent would be more effective elsewhere. One day I asked him if he thought he was having a broad impact in his current job, if he was really making a difference. From that day, a seed was planted. His mind opened up and he began to see the possibilities.

I often see talented men and women excelling in their careers while nursing a fierce discontent with where they are and what they're doing in their lives. They're not fulfilling their innermost desires. Furthermore, they're not serving and touching the people they are supposed to.

By August 2008, my friend took the steps to start his consulting business. As he developed, built, and worked toward launching his enterprise, I guided him every step of the way with positive assurance and reinforcement from my own example of success.

The naysayers will tell you that leaving a secure, highly compensated job in corporate America is crazy! But I believe pursuing a dream of entrepreneurship is a position of strength. It's a chance to create longevity and increased wealth. Just make sure the timing is right. If you are unemployed or underemployed, the timing is *right now!*

Being in business for yourself will offer you choices, and they'll be daunting, but opportunities will come your way for you to build your enterprise.

Inquiring minds may want to know, "How do I prosper from my power if I do not have any money to get my idea off the ground?"

Like Joseph, finding investors, people willing to financially back your business product or idea, is a better route since there are no payments to make and their investment is considered equity versus a debt. What's in it for investors? They earn their return off of your hard work.

If you achieve the results projected in your plan, they will receive income from profits or by the appreciation of their investment in your idea (like the parable of the talents). It's true that times are rough and investors are more conservative regarding what they will put their funds into today. However, a financially lucrative idea will attract investors and receive the funding it deserves.

Everybody wants to have shares in the next Google, BET, Facebook, or MySpace. There are investors everywhere who may be looking for the next great business idea in the hopes that it will become a huge success, thus earning them a big return.

You may be reading this and still thinking, "Well, I don't have any resources to start a business." Let me repeat that you don't need it. The only thing required is prayer, vision, faith, and a great plan. Like Joseph, if you have those things you can find the money—or shall I say, *the money will find you!*

Start small. If your idea is really sound and your product or service truly unique, believe me, somebody out there will partner with you. Even potential customers and family members are often willing to supply some needed funds to share in your success.

Remember, Joseph started as a consultant and ended with a retail empire. So stop worrying about money and concentrate on laying a strong foundation to build a thriving business. You'll discover that most things in life are funded by OPM—Other People's Money. You can do the same.

WEALTH BUILDING STARTS NOW

If you have the entrepreneurial fire, what are you waiting for? I coach and encourage those with potential and show them how to reach their goals. I also host workshops for ministers who desire to be tentmakers like the Apostle Paul, creating ventures that will allow them to be self-sufficient, and not burden the church, while securing economic security for their families.

Since the start of the recession, I have helped with the birthing of 40 new profitable businesses in the State of New Jersey through the Joy Community Development Corporation (Joy CDC), a 510(c)(3) affiliated with our church. I don't plan on stopping there. My goal is to help people create more.

I know what the start of a small enterprise can accomplish in society and in the lives of people. I witness it every day. V & R Cleaning is one such story.

Vincent Booker and his wife, Diane, are members in our church and were one of the many families impacted by unemployment. Both lost their jobs. Vincent was laid off by New Jersey Transit in 2008 and Diane's job was downsized the following year. I prayed with and encouraged them to step out in faith on the path of the unknown—entrepreneurship. They decided to take their meager savings, borrow some funds from family, and seek the help of our Community Development Corporation (CDC) to start their own commercial cleaning business.

The launch was a dream come true as well as a huge financial setback. The personal sacrifice was great since they had to put in a lot of work at first, with very little income in return. However, a year and a half later, V & R became a true success story.

The Bookers now have enough income to support their family. Had it not been for their courage to step out into the deep and take advantage of the opportunities CDC offered, they would have lost everything.

Like most Americans, their job loss could have started the domino effect of losing their health insurance, home, and everything that gave their family security. Now, the Bookers are experiencing liberty that two full-time jobs could have never given them. Owning their own business has been empowering. Today, with a full set of employees, the Bookers are changing many others by providing employment.

This is what America makes possible. They pursued wealth and the return has been gratifying. If you find yourself on the same path as the Bookers, why don't you venture out and secure the abundance your family deserves?

We are all blessed with unique skills and talents, many remaining unexplored or undeveloped. The next great idea or concept could be yours. If you desire to see God's power to get wealth activated, don't wait any longer to develop your 5-to-9 vision. Little dreams become big dreams.

Are you ready to begin?

Remember these wealth building secrets:

- You were born with power to attain wealth.
- The purpose of wealth is to establish God's covenant.
- Like Joseph, use what you have—your gifts, ideas, skills, and abilities will open many doors of opportunity.
- Wealth building is not 9 to 5, but 5 to 9.
- Create more than one income stream.
- Start by becoming an apprentice or find a mentor.
- Great ideas attract the resources to finance them.

WEALTH BUILDING SECRET #4

USE MONEY PROPERLY, OR LOSE IT

THERE ARE LAWS FOR WHICH WE MUST OPERATE IN ORDER TO PROSPER

Have you ever wondered why is it seems like the rich get richer and the poor get poorer? I know I certainly have.

It's mind boggling to think that there are only a small percentage of the world's richest people who give all glory to God for their wealth and who believe they are using it to expand His kingdom.

In searching the Scriptures, I stumbled upon a secret that I would like to share with you which explains this seemingly unfair phenomenon. First, let's start with this truth: the Almighty set the world into motion and there are laws for which His creation must operate in order to prosper.

Some of God's rules are exclusive to Christians, but

many apply to everyone. For example, God said, *"It is not good that man should be alone: I will make him a helper comparable to him"* (Genesis 2:18).

Therefore, anytime a man and woman, Christian or not, marry, in God's eyes it is good. In the larger view of things, every married man and woman have access to the blessing of the Lord for their union to experience goodness.

This passage does not specifically say that this decree of blessing is only to prosper Christians. Therefore, it is perfectly reasonable that you will find some "good" non-Christian marriages, because of this universal truth or law of God.

On the other hand, the promise of the 100-fold blessing decreed by Jesus in Mark 10:29-31 is *exclusive* to those who follow Jesus and live under the Gospel.

I believe the "secular" often apply biblical wisdom and operate in the prosperity of the laws of creation—in some case better than we Christians.

Perhaps Jesus would agree with me, if you read the Parable of the Unjust Servant in Luke 16 the way I do. Although there is much theological debate on the true meaning of this parable, one conclusion that can't be denied is Jesus' own interpretation of what the text means.

In the parable, the master commends his unjust steward for dealing very shrewdly with his financial matters: *"So, the master praised the dishonest manager for being clever. Yes, worldly people are more clever with their own kind than spiritual people are"* (verse 8, NCV). Yes, Jesus clearly labels the steward as unjust, meaning unrighteous and poor in character, but He bifurcates His view and also declares that perhaps believers should be more shrewd at handling finances so that they can work together and do more for the kingdom.

Here's another example. The Bible states, *"God loves a cheerful giver"* (2 Corinthians 9:7). While the context of this passage is encouraging Christians to properly sow into the ministry of their spiritual covering (who was the Apostle Paul at that time), this revelation is an all-encompassing law—that the Lord loves givers. But not just any kind; specifically those who give cheerfully.

If you've ever wondered why God delights in those who have this attitude, it is because *He* is a joyful, cheerful giver. Even more, the Creator always gives *first*. He didn't wait until we offered Him our trust and obedience before sending Jesus—that we might have a way out of sin (John 3:16). In truth, God is an "Eternal Philanthropist."

The most charitable givers in the world tap into the heart of the Lord, even if they might not know Him. Certain wealthy people become richer and richer because our benevolence reveals our *likeness* to God.

History records how the Almighty delivered the world and its wealth into the hands of ancient Persian kings, and the money was used to return God's remnant people—the Jews—back to Israel.

Some are convinced they will prosper just because they are Christians—in spite of the fact they may be violating universal laws established by the Creator. But if a Christian gives sparingly and grudgingly, while a non-believer exhibits liberal and cheerful giving, only one touches the heart of God—the unbeliever.

This may seem alarming, but it's true.

THE REAL REASON SEED IS ONLY FOR SOWERS

Now I want to dive into the deep part of the waters. Christians who do not have a heart to sow into God's work are embracing poverty.

Lack can create a severe catch-22 and cause many to lose hope that they will ever enter into abundance. Trust me—I've been there. In retrospect, it was not an issue of my faith, rather my ignorance of the laws of God. I remained in "lack" until I realized that the Lord had rules and guidelines for how I was to use the seed He had given me—no matter how little it was.

The Lord has the same rules for the person working at minimum wage as He does for the individual making millions. He expects us to use our seed properly, or we run the risk of losing it and continuing in the vicious cycle of poverty.

As we will see, how we manage our seed greatly influences whether or not we will experience the cycle of wealth. By seed, I mean money.

The Apostle Paul offered some sage advice on this topic. Writing to the believers at Corinth, he reminded them that a stingy planter receives a stingy crop, but a lavish planter reaps an abundant harvest.

Teaching on investing in the kingdom, Paul wrote, *"So let each one give as he purposes in his heart"* (2 Corinthians 9:7 NIV).

Notice who makes the decision—you do! And it is decided in your inner man.

Think of it this way: If I have a hard, unemotional spirit, it will be difficult for me to give—and the amount will probably be small. But if I possess a heart like God's, generosity will be reflected in everything I do, including my giving to my church, my family, the needy, and so on.

Then Paul made this life-changing statement: *"Now may He who supplies seed to the sower, and bread for food, supply and multiply the seed you have sown and increase the fruits of your righteousness"* (2 Corinthians 9:10).

The apostle is using an analogy or metaphor of seed and giving, but he's equating it to a financial gift. In other words, God provides an entrance ramp to the cycle of wealth to the person who has the heart, mind and ability to use it wisely.

Every believer has access to a money supply, and it doesn't come from your own storehouse or from the loan officer at your local bank. The text says that you have the passwords to an account at the Bank of Heaven!

Yes, God *"gives seed to the sower."* This means He is doing something at His own expense. God's bank is even better than Chase or Citibank. You never have to ask your heavenly Father for the seed to sow, since He is constantly bringing us to new entrance ramps on the cycle of wealth so that we might gain and bless the kingdom.

I pray this will enlighten those who feel the need to continually petition the Lord for money. Before begging for riches, there is first a work that must be accomplished. God dispenses His holy seed from heaven's storehouse to those who plan to use it properly—to sow.

What I am sharing is a wealth principle of the kingdom. As a result, we don't have to pray for the Lord to release wealth into our life; it has already been provided.

Remember, opportunity is constantly being dropped from above to bring people into the cycle of wealth. Freely! So once again, we find ourselves at the crux of the issue, perhaps it is not the lack of money, but the scarcity of *sowers* willing to do the right thing with the resource once it is received.

What would be the point of the Lord handing me a large sack of seed if I decided to pig out and make a meal of it all in one day? In God's wisdom, instead of simply handing us a fish, He teaches us *how* to fish, so we won't starve.

Now, in the Divine School of Agriculture, the Instructor gives us proven ways to use (plant) the seed He supplies and causes it to multiply. This is not *exclusive* to giving in church, but *inclusive* of such. The implications of this speak more to how and what we should faithfully do with the money or "seed" God has supplied.

The real question becomes, *do you know what to do with the seed?* Do you truly understand what sowing entails? Can God trust you with a large amount of seed, or not?

LACK ENDS, GOD BEGINS

Regardless of the amount of money (seed) God gifts to us, we must plant it. Remember, it is His seed and His ground. According to Scripture, *"The earth is the Lord's, and all its fullness, the world and all who dwell therein"* (Psalm 24:1). Every acre on this planet is His! This means that Christians ought to praise and give thanks to God for their families, jobs, homes, and clothes.

You might be college-educated and work hard to earn a living, but are we really so accomplished at what we do that we can claim no divine intervention or orchestration on our behalf? We are children of the Most High and we must first begin by acknowledging and attributing everything we have to Him—every cent.

It's not reasonable to complain that we were born with meager means; so were millions of others.

Paul continues this teaching by quoting Psalm 112, *"He has given to the poor"* (2 Corinthians 9:9).

Regardless how bleak our finances seem, God provides for those in need. To me, every assistance program, social support, overtime, and health benefit is nothing but the hand of God moving on the hearts of men and women to consider the poor. If we don't, who will?

I am reminded of the widow who only had "two mites"—a pittance—to place in the offering at the Temple (Mark 12:41-44). Jesus, wanting to open the eyes of those who were not presenting a sacrificial offering, said, *"Assuredly, I say to you that this poor widow has put in more than all who have given to the treasury; for they all put in out of their abundance, but she out of her poverty put in all that she had, her whole livelihood"* (Mark 12:43-44).

We also cannot forget the Shunammite widow who experienced abundance after she gave her last meal to the prophet Elisha (2 Kings 4). She had a choice to either eat what little food she and her son had left, or give it to God's servant. Thankfully, she made the right decision. Not only did this result in a never-ending supply of food, but her dying son was brought back to life (verses 32-37).

De'Andre Salter

As Christians, we are called to emulate those dedicated widows recorded in Scripture who demonstrated how investing just a little in the Lord's bank produces great dividends.

Satan's strategy is to fool people into believing that lack is insurmountable, but it is not. Our enemy is not financial lack, but wisdom lack. Since God has the whole world in His hands, even if I only have one dollar, He expects me to make wise choices and create something worthwhile with it.

The moment we are released from impoverished thinking, a new vista is opened up that leads to wealthy thinking. "Seed sowers" understand that a harvest doesn't happen overnight. However, if we plant today, we can expect a return later. Not only that, but my yield will be far greater than what I sowed.

At the Bank of Heaven, there are no applications to be completed or loan officers to meet. There's just one qualification for your approval: "Are you a seed sower?" It has nothing to do with the size of your account, or your credit rating. Are you willing to put the seed to work for the kingdom?

BRING YOUR SEEDS TO LIFE

Jesus gave an illustration that speaks to this point. He told the story of a wealthy landowner who was leaving on a lengthy journey and put his three servants in charge of everything he owned.

The story is buried in a series of parables where Jesus is expressing many things, but this one is a revelation of kingdom living. For those who are serving the Lord, it holds an even deeper meaning.

Here, Jesus is using terms of life and work, such as *talents*—pieces of money. He also speaks of *gain* in a financial sense and words such as *profit* and *unprofitable*.

The passage helps us understand how heaven views our stewardship on earth. In fact, Jesus could have used this same story in a corporate boardroom, giving a presentation on investing, and it would be understood clearly. For you and me, it provides a picture of how to become blessed in the kingdom.

The Bible tells us the landowner *"knew what each servant could do"* (Matthew 25:13 CEV). In other words, what he gave them had to do with his opinion of their individual abilities.

So, *"he handed five thousand coins to the first servant, two thousand to the second, and one thousand to the third"* (verse 15 CEV). Then he left the country.

As soon as the wealthy man departed, *"the servant with the five thousand coins used them to earn five thousand more"* (verse 16). The Bible doesn't tell us how he accomplished this—whether he started a business, bought wholesale and sold retail, or placed the cash in an interest bearing bank account. But he doubled his master's money.

Next, we learn, *"The servant who had two thousand coins did the same with his money and earned two thousand more"* (verse 17).

The money (seed) these first two men were given by the sower (in this case, the landowner), was used wisely. They produced more than they started with.

Now we come to the sobering part of the story: *"But the servant with one thousand coins dug a hole and hid his master's money in the ground"* (verse 18). One translation says that he *buried* the coins. Plain and simple, he hid the money with which he had been entrusted.

You might say, "He was just playing it safe." But that's not what his master thought.

As the narrative unfolds, *"Some time later the master of those servants returned. He called them in and asked what they had done with his money"* (verse 19). It was time to settle the accounts—and the landowner was anxious to hear the results.

The first servant said, *"Sir, you gave me five thousand coins, and I have earned five thousand more"* (verse 20).

The master replied, *"Wonderful...You are a good and faithful servant. I left you in charge of only a little, but now I will put you in charge of much more. Come and share in my happiness!"* (verse 21).

Notice the principle. When you take responsibility for small things, God will give you authority over *big* things. You must prove yourself to be trustworthy.

Next, the servant who had been handed two thousand coins reported how he had earned two thousand more. The joyous master's response was the same. In *The Message* translation, it reads *"Good work! You did your job well. From now on be my partner"* (verse 23).

Finally, the servant who had been given one thousand coins came in and told the landowner, *"Sir, I know that you are hard to get along with. You harvest what you don't plant and gather crops where you haven't scattered seed. I was frightened and went out and hid your money in the ground. Here is every single coin!"* (verses 24-25 CEV).

WHY THE RICH GET RICHER

To say that the master was upset puts it mildly. He was extremely angry and lashed out, *"You are lazy and good-for-nothing! You know that I harvest what I don't plant and gather crops where I haven't scattered seed. You could have at least put my money in the bank, so that I could have earned interest on it"* (verses 26-27).

The conclusion of the parable is difficult for many to understand, and at first glance it may seem unfair, but Jesus had a reason for sharing it.

The wealthy man said to the servant who hid the coins and produced no increase, *"Now your money will be taken away and given to the servant with ten thousand coins!"* (verse 28).

Oh my! The money from the one in poverty was handed over to the one in prosperity.

In our culture, we would hear howls of complaint from the servant who buried the money for safekeeping. "Lord, it seems like You should be giving me more, because my friends are already blessed and I am the one in need."

On the surface, it may seem unjust. People grouse, "Why are the poor not getting their fair share and the rich folk keep living high on the hog?"

In the story, Jesus added what some find even more confusing: *"Everyone who has something will be given more, and they will have more than enough. But everything will be taken from those who don't have anything"* (verse 29).

In today's vernacular, *the rich will get richer and the poor will get poorer.*

Why would Jesus use this particular illustration and draw such a conclusion? Here is, as they say, "the moral of the story."

If a man is penniless, and lives in fear of lack, consuming and hoarding everything, he is going to remain destitute! He will be locked into what we discussed in the first chapter of this book: a cycle of poverty instead of a cycle of wealth.

Speaking personally, there was a time the Lord couldn't trust me with a single dollar. When I was in my early 20s, I was more concerned with lifestyle than style of life. I wasn't the most generous person in the world, and eventually the way I was living got the best of me.

God blessed me with my first corporate job and it supplied my money (seed). What did I do? Like the unfaithful servant, I dug a hole for myself, using my seed for *me* and not putting it to work as God intended.

My "hole" lead to the unfortunate filing of a personal bankruptcy.

It was from this experience that God shared with me that I was the problem—He had been generous in giving me seed, but I had abused and squandered it.

I am happy to report today that since then, my standing in the Bank of Heaven (and the banks on earth) has a much higher score and I am a far better money manager.

In this parable, I believe Jesus was also speaking financially of those who have the wrong mentality and fail to grasp how kingdom stewardship works.

The man or woman who refuses to use the money God gives him or her rightly, will not only be bound by poverty, but even worse.

It is no coincidence that this entire account centers around money, while its spiritual meaning is about bringing souls into the kingdom.

Sowing of any kind has the objective of producing gain—investing, giving, education, and so on. Here, however, it is tied to being either profitable or unprofitable, fruitful or unfruitful.

GOD'S "BLESSING BUSINESS"

In a business sense, Jesus was communicating, "This is how you become blessed in My Father's corporation." If you look at the text, Jesus began the entire account by saying, *"The kingdom is also like what happened when a man went away and put his three servants in charge of all he owned"* (Matthew 25:14 CEV).

God also looks at your life and decides what He can trust you with. That's why there are degrees of blessing. In heaven's bank, each person is given a line of credit based upon their previous money management.

Coming to the Lord without first establishing your heart to be like those great widows, will only lower your approval amount.

While one may receive five bushels of divine "starter seed," others may only be given two or one.

Our heavenly Father is in the blessing business, so never become distracted or envious over someone else's means. Just improve your standing with the only bank that counts.

As a servant of the Lord, you have been richly blessed beyond measure. The power of a seed has been placed into your hands. It contains provision and increase, if you will only plant it in fertile soil.

INCREASE BY DECREASE

Let me help you even more to figure out how to work with kingdom rules to become wealthy.

There are only two ways to move ahead financially: make more money or spend less. It is universally accepted that it's usually harder to produce more income, but you can always control spending.

Often, we find ourselves buying compulsively; not because of a need or a want. We spend for deeper reasons that are hiding underneath the surface— insecurity, fear, unhappiness, lack of self-worth, etc. We give ourselves any excuse or justification to spend money, suffering more from our lack of knowledge pertaining to healthy financial habits.

If you dream of one day being rich, then you must start living like real rich people do. It may come as a surprise, but most of the wealthy are prudent, not as extravagant as the television shows and movies portray them.

Warren Buffet's philosophy has always been to live a simple and frugal life. He still lives in the same house he bought in the 1950s for $31,500, and, although he was a millionaire by his mid twenties, his kids had to work for their allowance and heard the word "no" more times than "yes" when they wanted something.[1]

There are smart, rich people all around you who care more about their long-term financial security than showing off their social status! They are operating in the truth of this parable—putting seed to work constantly and not hiding it in the ground.

The Wisdom of Joan

Let me encourage you with a living example of a person who knows how to handle seed.

Joan is married with three boys. By day, she works full-time at a bank and, by night, she runs a graphic design business as a sole proprietor. Joan works 20 hour days and says she only sleeps four hours a night. Maybe that would explain her Dunkin' Donuts addiction!

She brings home decent money, but scrutinizes everything she spends. Some have called her cheap, but if any of those people knew her, they'd discover that, like many who want to forge ahead, she is making sacrifices. She lives a frugal existence because she has priorities that largely outweigh frivolous comforts.

Joan does not need to drive a fancy car, so she doesn't. Her boys dress well, but not extravagantly. She enjoys activities, but keeps to her budget. All of her kids are educated at private schools.

How can she afford this on her salary? By using seed wisely. She carefully watches over the income from her side-business, and controls her expenses so that she can have what makes any mother happy—successful sons.

SOW INTO YOUR FUTURE

When it comes to your personal investments, put your funds in an opportunity that has the potential to bring a return. Examples would be starting a business, investing in a worthy idea, or buying a product at wholesale and selling it at a higher retail price for a profit.

Tom was at the top of his game; what you'd call a real estate titan in Florida. He started in the business with nothing but a desire to work. When he walked into his first job interview, he didn't have a college education, a real estate license, or any experience to compensate. He managed to convince the boss to hire him by reeling him in with an incredible story about how he'd sell a house. Talk about God supplying seed to the sower!

During good times, Tom was making top dollar in commissions at the peak of the season. Then, at the onset of the recent recession, his income was cut in half, as his industry began to suffer from the bust. In 2008, employees were laid off one by one, and the company's profits were going south.

Tom was running scared. His resources were dwindling, and no money was coming in. Real estate was his primary source of income, and now the bottom was falling out. How would he survive? How would he continue to provide for his family? Seed was running low, but remember, God gave it to him, and it had life.

As we sat together, talking about the declining housing market, I could see the concern in his eyes. It was just a matter of time when the money in the bank would turn into zero. I asked him if he knew what the term "vertical integration" meant.

What additional service could he offer in his wife's "house sitting" business? I suggested "pool cleaning."

By the look on his face, I could tell that it had never dawned on him that he could create a source of income through his wife's business. I encouraged him to recognize what God had already provided.

Tom wasn't quite sure how to begin and was uncomfortable subtracting any more money from the family's shrinking resources to start the new service, but he was a man rooted in faith and knew he had to take a leap to provide for his family.

It was time to sow that blessed seed of God; to work and wait in due time for the increase. So he decided to totally commit himself to his dream of achieving financial security again, and handed it over to God.

His trust in the Lord was such that he believed God would provide more seed along the way. So, he took the initial step.

Within the first quarter, Tom was cleaning 12

pools. He eventually doubled the number, and soon tripled it to what his wife was originally making. His business continues to grow and expand.

Tom attributes his success to his faith in God and using the seed properly. Even with his lifelong career crashing, his finances drying up, and his family's financial security in peril, God was providing entrance ramps on the cycle of wealth.

My friend Tom, a story of achievement, always remembers this verse: *"Delight thyself also in the Lord; and he shall give thee the desires of thine heart."* (Psalms 37:4)

SOW INTO SKILLS

God wants us to use seed for self-improvement. Ours is a very competitive, evolving world, one of global communication. In order to compete, our skills need to stay current and we should be constantly educating ourselves.

The quest for knowledge must never stop when you leave school; learning is a lifetime commitment. Education has been demonstrated to be not only the number one way to rise out of poverty but it is linked to all aspects of an improved quality of life. Sowing seed in this area will reap an amazing harvest.

This has proven to be true in the life of a woman named Monica. She was married at a very young age, and by 39, she and her husband were the proud parents of six children. Both worked to support their family. Monica was in retail for fifteen years and climbed her way up the ladder to an assistant store manager at Target, her pay capping between $35k-40k. Although the years were passing by and it seemed impossible, Monica never let go of her dream of becoming a lawyer. When Target downsized some of their stores, she found herself unemployed after a decade-and-a-half of loyalty.

She decided to consider her job loss a blessing and, against all odds, pursue her dream. I encouraged her as she began her journey to sow seeds into education. She enrolled at a local community college to finish her degree and used her unemployment checks to hold her over until she could work again. Government money was used as a means of subsistence, part of a bigger plan in bettering her life, and not a permanent lifestyle. Of course she should use whatever type of seed God supplies.

This wife and full-time mother took on additional courses to become a paralegal in order to gain experience in her field and supplement her income once she started law school.

Monica was incredibly focused and determined, keeping in mind the economic freedom that furthering her education would bring to her and the family. Today, Monica is well on her way. She is currently in law school. I was able to arrange an interview for her

at one of the top local law firms for a paid internship
—which, incidentally, pays more than her ending
salary at Target!

SOW INTO MINISTRY AND
GET THE "DETROIT" INCREASE

As I mentioned, your use of money should always
include investing in the kingdom—through your local
church. Far too many leave this work undone. It is a
common worldly practice to surprise a *CNN Hero* or
social do-gooder on a daytime talk show with a grand
gift of appreciation. But why do some Christians seem
so adverse to blessing a church or ministry with their
seed?

Remember, until that seed is put to work, its life is
aborted.

Paul the Apostle encouraged the church in Corinth
to remember what was written in the law of Moses:
*"You shall not muzzle an ox while it treads out the
grain"* (1 Corinthians 9:9). He was explaining that it
was the policy of heaven to sow material things
(money) into the ministry and those who supply it, in
return for the spiritual benefits (preaching, prayer,
counsel and deliverance) they receive.

**Again, the purpose of wealth building is kingdom
building.**

Shortly after attending a wonderful worship service,
the Lord arranged for me to cross paths with an

individual who wasn't particularly known, but God laid it upon my heart to sow into his ministry. It was as if the Lord whispered in my ear, "This is good ground."

So I wrote out a check and planted a seed into his life. The amount I gave was far less than what I had sown in other situations where God had not directed me. The only difference was, this time I was giving with the right spirit, at the direction of the Lord.

What happened next is beyond my ability to explain but it illustrates the life in seed. God unlocked something supernatural for me and my business began an amazing season of increase.

After sowing that seed, a gentleman from Detroit, with whom I only had a casual acquaintance, phoned me and we wound up in a business transaction together. In the process, he told me, "I don't know why I'm doing this. The whole deal is worth $75,000 and your cut is $30,000."

My heart was dancing at the very thought! God had increased the seed I had sown into the kingdom and that ministry, without a doubt.

The words he uttered next shocked me to my bones. "When the check arrives, don't send my portion. You just keep it all."

Dumbfounded, I asked, "The whole $75,000?"

He responded, "I feel you are going to be successful in business and I want you to use it for your enterprise. Then he added, "Now don't go and waste it all!" I guess he understood the stewardship of seed. You could have blown me over with a duck's feather! The man didn't even profess to be a Christian, but God moved him to bless me. Even more, he had no knowledge of the financial hardship I was in and how desperately I needed the money.

Upon the check's arrival, I showed it to my wife and exclaimed, "Baby, look at this!" We had never seen an amount that big in our lives.

This, and other experiences, have convinced me that if we use the seed properly and never risk losing it, God will do miraculous things for the prosperity of His children and the advancement of the kingdom.

Remember these wealth building secrets:

- God supplies seed to sowers.
- A seed that is not planted will remain lifeless, so use it properly or lose it.
- Make sure you plant into "good ground"—a business, skills, kingdom work and workers.
- Sow only into those things that will bring increase.

COMMIT YOUR HEART TO "WEALTH BUILDING FOR KINGDOM BUILDING"

GOD MAKES WEALTH DEPOSITS IN PEOPLE WHO ARE COMMITTED TO FINANCING THE GOOD NEWS

D id you have a piggy bank when you were a child? Perhaps you still own one. If so, how often do you put money in it?

Some folks, at the end of each day, take out all the bulky change from their pockets or purses, and drop in the coins. It may not seem like much, yet it's impressive how those pennies, nickels, dimes, and quarters quickly add up.

It's a wise idea to save for an unexpected emergency, whether you use a piggy bank or make regular deposits in a savings account. But we need to make sure that whatever treasure we are trying to build doesn't become the number one priority in our lives.

Jesus spoke to this issue in His sermon on the Mount of Olives. The disciple Matthew faithfully wrote the message He gave and it is found in chapters 5, 6, and 7 of the first book in the New Testament. Those who gathered to hear Christ sometimes heard teaching concerning living prosperously. Almost half of Matthew 6 is focused specifically on wealth and financial resources.

Jesus warned about being more concerned over what we accumulate and value on earth rather than what we deposit in the Kingdom. He said, *"Do not lay up for yourselves treasures on earth, where moth and rust destroy and where thieves break in and steal; but lay up for yourselves treasures in heaven, where neither moth nor rust destroys and where thieves do not break in and steal. For where your treasure is, there your heart will be also"* (Matthew 6:19-21).

What we stockpile in heaven is safe from corruption, and thieves. Jesus later cautioned about our evil adversary in particular when He said, *"The thief does not come except to steal, and to kill, and to destroy"* (John 10:10). He was speaking of Satan.

I don't think we can read this verse and assume the devil only wants to steal, kill and destroy our lives spiritually, without accepting that he desires to break us down slowly and have us lose our heart and soul. I further argue that his attacks on the finances of the followers of Christ are not only part of his plan but also a very *strategic* part. For if he succeeds in coaxing us into a cycle of poverty, he also robs the Kingdom of the potential financing it could receive from God-hearted believers whose support would lead to more people finding Christ. The last time I checked, thieves love money more than any other "score"!

There's a distinct difference between a thief and a robber: a thief uses deception while a robber uses force.

The devil is not as powerful as some would give him credit. His major weapon is to trick you into giving up, or to entice you with what he knows you have a weakness for. It's your Achilles' heel. Thieves use lies, deception, and trickery to obtain their gain. Satan is a master thief.

Financially, he may even tempt you with a guilt trip that has you handing out money to a loved one who just keeps squandering it away.

His deceit also leaves you wondering, "Why don't God's promises work for me?" The reason Satan can steal wealth from you is because the money was never committed to the Kingdom in the first place.

Have you ever received a paycheck and a couple of days later, you shook your head in disbelief, saying, "Where did it all go? What happened to my money?" It's because the biggest thief of all time, the devil, may have stolen from you:

- He stole it at the movie rental kiosk.
- He stole it when you made a late payment on your credit card and they raised your interest rate.

- He stole it when you signed up for a thousand cable channels you never watch.
- He stole it when you used an off-brand ATM machine and they charged you $3 for a $20 bill.
- He stole it when you didn't consider the odds and bought a lottery ticket.
- He stole it when you ordered an extra large mocha latte instead of a regular cup of coffee.
—and the list is long.

What a contrast from what you place in God's storehouse. When you give into the Kingdom and have a heart that God blesses with the power to attain wealth, your treasure is protected.

It also means you can face the devil head-on, and with confidence look him in the eye and declare, "When the Lord blesses me, there's nothing you can do about it!"

Your piggy bank can include so much more than money. There are countless ways to increase your heavenly account. For instance, helping to feed the hungry, visiting someone in a hospital, being a friend to a person who is lonely, bringing cheer to someone who is sad and depressed, or forgiving a friend who has hurt you.

THE TWO KINGDOMS

Please hear my heart; wealth is not good for

everyone. Some can't handle it. We see headlines practically every day of the rich and famous who are either entering rehab, losing their families, committing suicide, or dying of a drug overdose.

Las Vegas and Atlantic City are filled with individuals who are gambling to cope with the stresses of life—and their slot machine or blackjack losses just perpetuate the problem.

The only true measure of the amount of wealth you possess is found in your heart. Remember, there are two kingdoms—the earth's and God's. You are either living by the principles of one or the other. If you try to mix the two, you're headed for disaster.

Jesus asked this important question: *"What will it profit a man if he gains the whole world, and loses his own soul?"* (Mark 8:36).

If our heart is not conditioned toward the things of God, we subvert His divine plan. When believers start placing material things at the top of their list, discipleship and evangelism takes a back seat and the Kingdom doesn't expand.

Some men and women have trouble handling a blessing. When they move into a better home or drive a bigger car, their attitude changes. Suddenly, instead of offering to pick up people and bring them to church, they're out for a leisurely Sunday drive. Rather than thinking of others, they have new priorities.

The Lord is watching and asking, "Where is your heart?"

Avoid Achan's Sin

Immediately after pointing out the distinction between laying up things of value here on earth rather than placing them in God's hands, Jesus gave this example: *"The lamp of the body is the eye. If therefore your eye is good, your whole body will be full of light. But if your eye is bad, your whole body will be full of darkness. If therefore the light that is in you is darkness, how great is that darkness!"* (Matthew 6:22-23).

The Lord is telling us that the way we view things, our perception, makes a huge difference. Obviously, He wants us to *see* the treasure principle.

Since your eyes are the windows into your inner man, if you open them wide and believe, you will be filled with knowledge and light. But if you are squinting in greed and distrust, your body becomes cloaked in darkness.

The contrast in both passages—between heaven and earth, light and darkness—is obvious. The *good* eye has healthy vision and sees God's way of doing things.

When you have heavenly sight, you can walk into a room full of people and make the right connections. But with a dark or diseased eye, it is much like having glaucoma or cataracts. Your vision is blurred, and you may be mistaken about what you think you see and, as a result, make some terrible choices or connections.

When Joshua and the children of Israel finally

125

crossed the Jordan and marched into the Promised Land, God gave them wealth, starting with the conquering of Jericho. But the Lord told Joshua to notify the people, *"By all means abstain from the accursed things, lest you become accursed...and make the camp of Israel a curse"* (Joshua 6:18). He was speaking of gold and silver which were *"consecrated to the Lord"* and should be reserved for His treasury (verse 19).

Well, there was a man named Achan who disobeyed and hid some plunder from Jericho under the rug in his tent. But God was watching and His anger burned.

The next battle took place at the city of Ai. Joshua sent an army of several thousand men, but they were quickly routed by the enemy and had to flee back to Jericho.

Joshua was humiliated and, in anguish, cried before the Lord. God told him there was a cursed item in their midst—and that was the reason for their crushing defeat.

Immediately, Joshua called for every tribe to be throughly searched. When they came to the tribe of Judah, Joshua pointed to Achan and asked, "What have you done?"

Achan confessed. And when Joshua went into the tent and pulled up the rug, there lay the stolen gold and silver. It was laid out for the children of Israel to see, and Achan was killed with stones and thrown into a fire.

The next battle for Ai had the opposite outcome, and Israel won a major victory.

The message of this story and the teaching of Christ on the Mount of Olives is that you cannot have a "dark eye" and a deceitful heart and expect godly wealth and success.

Therefore, before you pray for wealth, consider if you can be trusted with it. Do not brag to your friends concerning your trustworthiness or value your self-opinion, but consider if God can trust you with the wealth of the world.

GENEROUS SIGHT

Jesus emphasized that if your eye is good, *"your whole body will be full of light"* (Matthew 6:22), because a healthy eye is a generous eye. As I mentioned earlier, generosity is one of the keys to wealth that applies to both believers and unbelievers.

I will admit that some miserly people accumulate money, but their greed eventually comes back to bite them. Generous people, however, grow even *more* wealthy.

Our heavenly Father set the ultimate example: *"For God so loved the world that He gave..."* (John 3:16). The reason He gave His Son is because He believed you are worth something—and have eternal value.

You see, we give out of what we firmly believe and totally trust.

The opposite of a healthy eye is one that is

127

diseased—an eye that is selfish. For instance, I have encountered people who have been helped greatly by others but once back on their feet, have never returned the favor—or shown the slightest hint of generosity.

If you have achieved any level of success, it's not too late to think about those individuals who extended a helping hand. You'll never know what a handwritten note or a phone call to such a person will mean.

- Who is that person who spoke encouraging words when you needed them most?
- Who is that school teacher who told you that you have a special talent?
- Who is that relative who said, "I believe in you"?
- Who is that friend who expressed, "I feel you're really going to make it"?
- Who is that individual who gave you your first job opportunity?"
- Who is that co-worker who always offers a word of encouragement when you're having a tough day?
- Who is that Christian friend who lifts your spirit, saying, "I've been praying for you"?

It is never too late to let them know how much you appreciate them.

Everything about God's Kingdom can lead to a life of abundance, but when it pertains to finances, we have to make a choice. As Jesus declared, *"No one can serve two masters; for either he will hate the one and love the other, or else he will be loyal to the one and despise the other. You cannot serve God and mammon"* (Matthew 6:24). The word "mammon" means money, wealth, or greed.

If you really want to unpack the concept of this, I suggest you read Dr. Kenneth Ulmer's book, *The Power of Money.*

Believers must reach the place where they should not be able to tolerate unethical ways of doing business, and feel uncomfortable with the "grey areas" of life.

True Kingdom people never take advantage of others. Instead they lay up riches by demonstrating God's love to a hurting world.

If you try to serve two masters, you'll soon discover that double vision is costly—and may cause you to have more accidents than you can count.

DON'T WORRY, GOD HAS A PLAN FOR YOUR FINANCIAL WELL BEING

In the same message where Jesus connected our treasure to our heart, and that we must serve God instead of money, He gave this example:

Therefore I say to you, do not worry about your life, what you will eat or what you will drink; nor about your body, what you will put

129

on. Is not life more than food and the body more than clothing?

Look at the birds of the air, for they neither sow nor reap nor gather into barns; yet your heavenly Father feeds them. Are you not of more value than they?

Which of you by worrying can add one cubit to his stature?

So why do you worry about clothing? Consider the lilies of the field, how they grow: they neither toil nor spin; and yet I say to you that even Solomon in all his glory was not arrayed like one of these.

Now if God so clothes the grass of the field, which today is, and tomorrow is thrown into the oven, will He not much more clothe you, O you of little faith? (Matthew 6:-25-30).

This hits us right where we live! What's sitting in our pantry and hanging in our closet?"

I like the way *The Message* translation interprets this:

If you decide for God, living a life of God-worship, it follows that you don't fuss about what's on the table at mealtimes or whether the clothes in your closet are in fashion.

There is far more to your life than the food you put in your stomach, more to your outer appearance than the clothes you hang on your body.

Look at the birds, free and unfettered, not tied down to a job description, careless in the care of God. And you count far more to him than birds (verses 25-26).

In our consumer, media-driven culture, it seems everybody is eyeing us from head to toe to see if we are keeping up with the latest trends and fashions.

If we're not careful, we can live our entire life *externally,* instead of having a heart for God. We then find ourselves seeking money, power, and celebrity, forgetting the aim I have been emphasizing in this entire book—wealth building for Kingdom building. When you grab hold of this principle you will find that your heart is in tune with God's.

When our heart matches His, we can shed some of our earthly burdens. This is why Jesus questioned why we are so anxious about our needs when other creatures He also made simply wake up in the morning and trust God's ecosystem. Birds don't lose sleep wondering if there will be a fresh worm in the morning!

If you journey through life, taking each step with doubt and fear, you are hurting yourself physically, spiritually, and emotionally. But there is an answer. You can start the turn-around by greeting each new morning proclaiming, "God made this day for me to prosper!"

Jesus confirms this: *"Your heavenly Father knows that you need all these things"* (Matthew 6:32).

Then Jesus comes to the grand conclusion of His message on wealth and provision: *"But seek first the kingdom of God and His righteousness, and all these things shall be added to you"* (verse 33).

Please notice. In His teaching, Jesus does not say, "Don't seek wealth." I feel the need to tred carefully here, since so many people desire to interpret Jesus' words as encouraging poverty. (I will address the Jesus poverty issue in Secret #7). Instead, He states what seems like the other bookend to the power to get wealth passage in Deuteronomy 8—the primary target for every Christian on earth: *"Seek first the kingdom of God."* There is no mention of what we are to search for second, third, fourth, or fifth—because nothing else matters. If the Kingdom is first, everything else falls into line. This proves that He wants people who He can bless to expand this divine empire.

The dilemma for most individuals is that they search for a *promotion* first, or a bigger *paycheck*—any objective instead of the one that will give them the most abundance on earth and the riches of eternity. The first step is a piggy bank heart—one God can trust with more money than the wealthy King Solomon of old.

Sadly, many place far too much emphasis on *"all these things shall be added unto you"* and ignore the prerequisite: *"Seek first the kingdom."* No doubt, those material things that Jesus speaks of can and will be added, but for what aim if not Kingdom building? The word "seek" is a verb, which means action is required. It's also in the *present imperative* tense, letting us know that we must be continually seeking—in this case, how to have God's heart and gain wealth for the Kingdom.

THE "RIGHTEOUSNESS" FACTOR

There is another secret to God's blessing that I don't want to gloss over. Jesus continued, "*...and His righteousness*" (Matthew 6:33).
This means:

• Seeking His righteousness in your giving.
• Seeking His righteousness in your stewardship.
• Seeking His righteousness in your investing.
• Seeking His righteousness in your spending.

We will have rewards in heaven, but if we follow God's plan, our needs will also be supplied on earth. Instead of chasing after material "things," we must start running toward the spiritual reasons for material gains.

Our power to attain wealth lies in using our God-given abilities. When we begin to get our "moral man" in order and our hearts are changed, we will be able to seize the *right* opportunities God opens up for us. But we still have to work. Money doesn't grow on trees and won't fall to the earth like apples.

In a society and culture that has become "government dependent," it's time for believers to become "God dependent"—by putting His Kingdom first. Then, by working *His* plan, the benefits will follow.

Even when the children of Israel made it to the Promised Land, some were still hanging onto their old idols, but Joshua told them it was time to make a decision. He demanded, *"Choose for yourselves this day whom you will serve"* (Joshua 24:15 NIV).

Fortunately, Joshua practiced what he preached and made the right choice, declaring, *"As for me and my house, we will serve the Lord"* (verse 15).

If we decide to go our own way, we take all the pressure off of our heavenly Father. He doesn't have to bless us or add *"all these things"* to our lives. But when we seek the Kingdom *first*, the Lord has a promise to keep.

The message of wealth building is clearly scriptural, but the wealth we are to receive must come through the hands of God, not via our own schemes and devices.

A misinterpretation of what the Bible says about money and wealth can result in a "Give me" mentality. Even adults can sound like spoiled, petulant children. For a moment, stop and ask yourself, "Is the Kingdom first in my heart?"

Please understand, the Lord wants you to have all the things He mentions in this passage, including food and clothing, but God demands that nothing be given higher priority than Himself. Remember, in the first of the Ten Commandments, the Almighty declared, *"You shall have no other gods before Me"* (Exodus 20:3). And He added, *"I, the Lord your God, am a jealous God"* (verse 6).

TREASURES TODAY, OR JUST TOMORROW?

Some read Matthew 6 and conclude, "Jesus is only talking about the riches of eternal life; it has nothing to do with wealth on earth."

Hold on! When the Lord speaks of treasures being where your heart is, it includes both the here and the hereafter.

When Christ promised, *"these things will be added to you,"* He was teaching about more than a spiritual blessing—but that which is tangible and you reach out and touch today.

Jesus made this remarkable statement: *"Mark my words, no one who sacrifices house, brothers, sisters, mother, father, children, land—whatever—because of me and the Message will lose out. They'll get it all back, but multiplied many times in homes, brothers, sisters, mothers, children, and land—but also in troubles. And then the bonus of eternal life!"* (Mark 10:29 MSG).

He was letting you know that no matter what you sacrifice, it will be worth it all. You won't lose out. Your life will be a testimony to the world that God is on your side.

Abundance CAN be a supernatural byproduct of seeking Christ and His righteousness.

Does this mean everything will be smooth sailing? Absolutely not. Jesus stated that what we receive will also be multiplied *"in troubles"* (verse 30).

When God pours out His favor on you, people can react with a spirit of jealousy and gossip. They may even blame you for not helping them. So do not be surprised at persecution; just consider the source.

Jesus said this multiplication will take place *"in this present age"* (verse 30 NIV). Eternal life is just icing on the cake!

Asking, seeking, and knocking are central to having a piggy bank heart God can trust. That's why Jesus gave this divine formula: "Ask, and it will be given to you; seek, and you will find; knock, and it will be opened to you" (Matthew 7:7).

It's interesting that the first letter of those three words—Ask, Seek, Knock—spell ASK.

Modeling a heart after God starts with prayer (asking), then expectation (seeking), and finally, work and action (knocking).

Today, make certain you are laying up eternal treasures. This is possible when you have a piggy bank heart and are making Kingdom deposits that will never perish.

Remember these wealth building secrets:

- We must be more concerned with what we deposit in God's Kingdom than what we accumulate on earth.
- Don't let Satan steal from you through deceitful reasoning.
- It is impossible to serve God and money at the same time. But it is possible to have your money serve God.
- Do not be anxious over earthly provisions. The Lord knows exactly what you need.
- Seek first God's Kingdom and His righteousness, and discover His plan for your personal well being.
- What the Lord promised will be yours today, and for eternity.

WEALTH BUILDING SECRET #6

DISCOVER THE KEYS TO MAKING BETTER DECISIONS

YOU WERE BORN WITH A FREE WILL AND THE POWER TO CHOOSE. HOW YOU USE THAT POWER MAKES THE DIFFERENCE BETWEEN ABUNDANCE AND POVERTY, SUCCESS AND FAILURE

What was the worst decision you ever made? Perhaps you've tried to erase it from your mind, but you can't—because every choice we make affects us for a lifetime.

To narrow it down, what was the worst *financial* decision you ever made? For many it was buying something they couldn't afford in order to maintain a certain image. Perhaps it was losing money by investing in some hair-brained scheme or wasting away a small windfall.

We all have stories of failing to take the right fork in the road when we had the chance. Each of us has taken unfortunate exits on the cycle of wealth. For instance, according to *The Motley Fool Investment Newsletter*, if you had scraped together $2,000 to buy Pepsi Cola stock in 1980, it would be worth over $200,000 today.

Of course, you have to understand the axiom that money makes money, and decide to let your investment grow on its own timetable and momentum.

Decisions affect our relationships, too. A girl in college had two classmates who were competing for her love: one was ruggedly handsome, while the other was a geek. She decided to marry for looks—but soon found out the guy was bone lazy and they were eventually arguing over the lack of money. The geek, however, turned out to be a high-tech multi-millionaire.

Bad decisions can certainly come back to haunt you.

One of my college friends turned down an invitation to take a job with a fledgling start-up company called Microsoft. Instead, he joined a venture capital firm and was making top dollar compared to other college grads at the time.

Six months later, Microsoft went public on the stock market, and practically every employee became an instant millionaire—including receptionists and secretaries.

My friend kicked himself over and over for making such a mistake.

Like my friend, there are many decisions that we wish we could make all over again, only to discover the reality that we cannot.

A PLAN FOR YOUR SURVIVAL

Here is the simple message of this chapter: **God wants His children to make wise financial decisions so we won't suffer the poverty that results from foolish choices.**
Please understand; the Lord is not sitting in heaven with a notepad, waiting for you to mess up. He just wants you to follow His plan to stay on the right path. Just look at the order of creation. God first made the water, then the land, then man. Otherwise, Adam would have drowned! He also created trees with leaves before man; without them, what would Adam have covered himself with after he sinned?" This is to say that there is an order to the making of things, and it also applies to creating wealth.

If you ask 100 people, "How many of you want to be wealthy?" You would likely get 100 hands raised high. If then you asked, "How many are willing to make all the necessary sacrifices, practice self-denial, live with delayed-gratification, drive through long, purposeful, productive hours, experience seasonal loneliness, press forward in spite of persecution, etc.?" Perhaps quite a few would hesistate, then lower their hands.

People are generally idealistic, especially in an age where we desire instant rewards and 15 minutes of fame by posting a selfie! However, financial wealth doesn't usually happen that quickly; it occurs as a result of intentional, purposeful, willful, and astute financial decision making. Our resources must be carefully managed if we are to experience wealth —and this is no easy task. We are surrounded by bad financial options, making it easy to blow it!

FOUR BAD DECISIONS
YOU SHOULDN'T MAKE

In chapter 3, I shared the story of how Joseph, the son of Jacob, had a dream that his brothers would one day bow down to him. Let's not over spiritualize the dream—it was basically about how rich and powerful Joseph would be, and how impoverished his brothers would become. It was God's way of giving Joseph a vision before He gave him provision.

God knew Joseph needed something to carry him through the pit, the prison, and into the palace. On the other hand, when Joseph shared his wealth dream with his brothers, they reacted in a way that teaches us much about how bad decision-making can lead us away from purpose and prosperity.

Bad Decision #1: Joseph's brothers allowed their envy and jealousy to drive their conduct.

From the time Jacob gave Joseph a coat of many colors, the brothers *"hated him and could not speak a kind word to him"* (Genesis 37:3). And when he revealed his dream of them being subservient to him, *"they hated him all the more"* (verse 8).

In hindsight, his brothers would have saved themselves much heartache if they had embraced Joseph's vision instead of giving into their envy and insecurity. Jealousy of others will always lead us to bad financial decisions. In fact, the whole idea of "keeping up with the Joneses" speaks to a person who buys far too many material things in order to compete with the possessions of someone else.

Are you driving a luxury car simply because you want to feel superior in the eyes of others? I have owned luxury vehicles and non-luxury vehicles and here is a truth I have learned: they both get you to a destination using four wheels! The extra money spent for status or profile could and should be better used to finance your power to get wealth which we spoke of in chapter 3. Or it should be invested as we discussed in chapter 4. In other words, envy leads us straight to the exit sign on the cycle of wealth. We can all do much better if we avoid the temptation of jealousy.

The problem with coveting is that it is a dream killer. As in the case of Joseph's brothers, we can be destroying the vision of a person God has sent our way to help us enter the cycle of wealth—just like Abraham helped Lot to do.

In my first corporate job, there was a manager who wasn't particularly fond of me because he felt I was too rough around the edges. I later discovered that he was envious of the fact that as an intern, I had favor with the local branch manager two years earlier (who was now his boss), and he resented my access to power. I couldn't help it that God opened doors that no man could close!

One day I shared a presentation that I developed to help the whole company increase sales and I asked for his support to pitch it to the corporate-suite executives in our home office. In fact, my idea spurred an open competition where many were invited to present their best ideas to the big-wigs. He told me, "I don't think your background is conducive to your public speaking skills." I think that was a politically correct way of telling me, *because you grew up in an urban landscape perhaps this is a bit over your head.*

So, like Joseph, I shared my dream with his superior, my benefactor, his boss. I gained the branch managers' support to make this pitch.

By the way, I also confided to my branch manager about working for a person who was trying to sabotage my career. I learned a valuable lesson from the branch manager that day: ignore envy and jealousy or you will suffer at the hands of it!

So, to make a long story short, I was told that I nailed the presentation. The C-Suite loved my proposal and said it was the most innovative and best idea they had heard in years. They were shocked that I *spoke* so well. I guess it was the preacher in me being prepared.

Well, nothing stays the same in corporate America. About seven years later, I had left that company to take a bigger executive position in Chicago. We posted a job opening for a new team member, and guess who applied? Yes, my old department manager who had been fired from our prior company due to malfeasance.

Please understand, my vision for the earlier corporation wasn't about me self promoting myself or being a star, I just wanted the support of my team leader. The man's envy caused him to miss an opportunity to have his name attached to a huge product, and now he found himself in need of a job.

Jealousy inevitably leads us to bad decisions. They cause us to make extremely poor financial choices, or they make us—like my old department manager—a dream killer, who might be stomping on a vision that could one day prosper him.

The world is full of negative people, pessimistic naysayers, and cynics. They're everywhere. We cross paths with them at work, in the streets, in our neighborhoods, schools, intimate circles, in the media, even in the pews of our churches. Many times, we don't need to look further than our own family.

Joseph's brothers of today, the dream killers, are skeptics, and they often do not have a vision themselves. They're jealous, secretly envious, and covet our aspirations. Usually, their sole aim is to discourage everyone around them and tear down the hopes and expectations others have built for themselves. They're like the teacher who yells at the student, "You'll never succeed," or the "well-meaning" friend that gently warns, "You're out of your mind for thinking you can achieve that."

Perhaps you've heard one of those comments along the way. Instead of offering encouragement and support, today's descendents of Joseph's brothers will list every reason under the sun why your quest for wealth is foolish:

- "You're a single-parent mom. How are you going to go back to school to get a master's degree?"
- "You can't start a business. Who is going to watch your kids?"
- "You don't have any money!"
- "Your credit is too bad. Nobody's going to lend you anything!"

Misery loves company. Dream killers carry an infectious disease like a plague, and if we don't protect ourselves, we'll catch it too. We have to guard our vision and be careful not to tread upon the hopes and ambitions of others—your blessing may be in their dream.

Bad decision#2: Joseph's brothers threw away their blessing.

First, the siblings hated Joseph because he had a vision and a dream—and they didn't. So when he came out to the field where they were working, they plotted to kill him, but the oldest brother, Reuben, said, "No, let's just cast him into this pit."

Then, as the Bible records, *"they sat down to eat a meal"* (Genesis 37:25).

Think about that for a moment. You throw you brother in a hole with no food and water, and you start eating in front of him! This gives us a glimpse of the cold, calloused hearts of Jacob's other sons, caused by their sin of jealousy.

Now the brothers had another problem. They had just thrown their blessing into a pit. This was the most significant opportunity they ever had, and they didn't even recognize it.

Perhaps we should examine if we have ever cast aside a blessing God has sent us. I know I certainly have.

Here is a secret within the secret: **God usually blesses us through people, not things.** When was the last time you saw bread literally rain from heaven? In the wilderness, manna came down because of God's relationship with a man named Moses. So it was a *person* who interceded for those who received the Lord's favor. Likewise, now as heirs, we are blessed by Abraham.

Salvation did not just happen by osmosis, it only took place when God became Man. I guess you could say God is a "people person."

Earlier I discussed how to use the seed, now I want to encourage you to see others as God's provision. This is not narcissistic, it is spiritual.

Our heavenly Father blesses us through people, places, and things, usually in that order. Yes, He will direct us to go to a place, like when He told Abraham about a land of milk and honey. He can also bless us with five loaves and two fish, but we will be hard pressed to find Him doing that without using an individual to be part of the transaction.

Perhaps this is why Jesus says that the greatest commandments are to love God and love people (Matthew 22:35-40). Everything in the kingdom seems to work along those lateral and vertical dimensions as they align with the axises of these two command-ments.

The financial application of this is significant since you will most likely need a person or people, to help you finance your advanced education, invest in your start-up idea, help you climb out of debt, fight for your pay increase at work, approve your bank loan, endorse your new product, or buy into your grand idea.

I pray you are seeing the big picture. You will need those God sends your way to be part of your wealth building plan.

Regardless of what anyone says, no one achieves wealth by themselves, they all have help from others. In fact, there is no such thing as a self-made man. There had to be a person who helped along the way—usually more than one. But even if it's only God and you, anything is possible.

I fear that many are throwing their provision in the pit. Like Joseph's brothers, they exit from the cycle of wealth simply because they can't learn to relate to their fellow man. Be honest, how many individuals has the Lord sent your way that you've tossed aside because they "rubbed you the wrong way" or had a different socio-economic background from yours?

One of the best decisions I ever made was to put into practice treating everyone equally—you never know who God is sending to bring His blessings.

When I was working in corporate America, before I went "entrepreneural" and struck out on my own, I learned to speak to every person in the organization with respect, because they are special in God's sight.

So I made the effort to treat everybody alike, from the top dogs to the clerks and receptionists.

I could tell you numerous stories of those who exhibited a haughty attitude. In some cases, the employees who they ignored became their superiors —and they didn't forget how they were once dealt with.

I remember being rebuked by my management peers because I took mail room employees to lunch for no reason whatsoever. Even when I became part of the senior executive team, I would still enjoy spending time hanging out at McDonald's with those doing the grunt work, talking sports, politics, or whatever.

You never know who you are befriending that is there to bless you. The Bible is full of stories where God uses the most unexpected people to bless His remnant.

Perhaps you can enter the cycle of wealth by riding in the car of someone else who knows the way or who is just willing to join you on the journey.

Remember, the Lord blesses people through people—of all types—to bring favor to your life.

Bad decision #3: Joseph's brothers lived for today, only to starve tomorrow.

Suddenly, one of the brothers thought of a better idea: "Let's sell Joseph for money, because he is surely worth a shekel or two."

When a camel caravan of merchants came passing by, they pulled him out of the ground and sold him for 20 shekels—about $6 in today's money. And the Ishmaelites carried him off to Egypt.

Let me get this right; they sold their provision for a pittance. They had no idea that 13 years later they would be starving because of a famine in the land

—while Joseph rose to prominence, becoming one of the most influential and richest men in Egypt.

Any good investor will advise you, "Never sell a good stock too soon." This is also God's lesson. We must not sell our future for a temporary pleasure right now.

I certainly understand the pressures today's world inflicts. But be careful: the decisions you make now could result in worries far worse tomorrow.

Like Joseph's brothers, we don't know "the rest of the story"—that God had a plan which would eventually make Joseph the governor of all Egypt.

When Joseph interpreted the dream of Pharaoh, he said, "There will be seven years of plenty and seven years of drought—so store up ample wheat now if you want to make it through the coming dry seasons." Because of his wise prediction, Pharaoh put Joseph in charge of all the grain.

Joseph was going to be a man of riches and success no matter what; and his brothers would have had an easier life if they had been able to avoid some of their bad decisions.

Choices that short-change our future by getting us out of financial trouble today will always make it worse in the end. Never try to convince yourself otherwise.

Joseph's uncle Esau also sold his birthright for a pittance, and it did not turn out well for him either. No matter what financial decisions you must make, never make the one where you sell out your future. I'd rather endure a financial drought today than live in lack forever.

Bad decision #4: Joseph's brothers lived in denial about their present circumstances.

They decided to lie their way out of trouble. Their deceit began when they smeared some blood on their brother's robe and told their father, "Look at this. Joseph was killed by some wild animals."

Later, when they had to journey to Egypt to find food, they bowed low before the governor (Joseph) and lied again. When Joseph tested them by suggesting they might be spies, they replied, *"No...we are honest men"* (Genesis 47:10-11).

Joseph was not fooled. How honest are you being about your financial situation? Do you see that you might have a spending problem? Using your credit cards too much? Do you agree that envy and jealousy have led you to poor financial management? Have you looked in the mirror and noticed that you have put people in the pit that were sent to bless you?

Living in denial about our finances does not make the lack disappear. We can't fool Visa, Amex, or MasterCard; they know the truth. They are laughing at the interest profits Americans hand them every day. An article in *The Atlantic Magazine* argues that even in the suburbs, people are living paycheck-to-paycheck since 33 percent of households have very meager liquid savings. The author called them "the middle class poor."[1]

Your wealth will not change unless you begin with an accurate assessment of what you might be doing to keep yourself out of the cycle of wealth. I hope this book is helping to identify those negatives and reveal to you a better path.

For every action there is a reaction, and for every bad financial decision there will be a consequence.

The wealth choices we made yesterday affect our financial situation today—and whether we like it or not, we have to deal with the fallout. And the choices we make today affect our tomorrow.

Every financial decision leads to either a poverty problem or a wealth privilege. If you take the wrong path, it will lead to trouble. Consequently, you'll find yourself having to deal with the earlier wealth mistakes.

Your poor financial assessment creates the initial problem. What starts as a money snowball can turn into a poverty avalanche that comes barreling down the mountain! And soon you find yourself buried in debt and lack.

But the right financial decisions can result in wealth privilege—the kind that encourages you to apply the principles found it this book.

"GOD DECISIONS" ARE "GOOD DECISIONS"

There is a passage in Proverbs we cannot afford to overlook. King Solomon wrote: *"Evil pursues sinners, but to the righteous, good shall be repaid. A good man leaves an inheritance to his children's children, but the wealth of the sinner is stored up for the righteous"* (Proverbs 13:21-22).

These verses are often quoted in prosperity circles to inspire those in the pew to get excited about hitting the wealth jackpot in a church service through "giving to get," but this speaks to something far greater.

What the writer is getting at is this: if I am living by the world's standards, making unrighteous decisions, especially financial ones, trouble is going to find me. But for men and women who are committed to Christ and doing what is right in His sight, something marvelous is on the horizon.

In this text, the Lord promises to reward good decision making. Remember, since God desires wealthy Christians to finance His kingdom, He is certainly going to honor those who practice integrity and stewardship.

The same passage speaks of the transfer of wealth from the sinner to the saint. Let me offer this word of caution: this does not happen just because we claim it.

There is spiritual wisdom which details how wealth is transferred. This may take place because of a person who makes some foolish choices, driven by greed and materialism—and their holdings become the property of a faithful steward who has put these wealth building secrets into practice.

This wisdom is for those who are serious about making the proper choices, ones who are in the right position to prosper from the poor financial decisions of others.

Let God guide every decision you make. With His help, you will experience abundance beyond measure.

Remember these wealth building secrets:

- God blesses people through people.
- Avoid "dream killers" who try to destroy your vision.
- Never allow jealousy to drive your decisions.
- The choices we make today affect our tomorrow.
- Be totally honest about your economic situation.
- Every financial decision leads to either a poverty problem or a wealth privilege.
- Only "God Decisions" are "Good Decisions."

BELIEVE YOU CAN BE WEALTHY

*REJECT THE IDEA THAT FINANCIAL
WEALTH IS NOT POSSIBLE FOR YOU—
THE BIBLE TEACHES OTHERWISE*

Some men and women come from a tradition that believes money should have no prominent platform in Christian teaching. They are of the opinion that to be a true Christian you must suffer with Christ—including financially. They like to quote Jesus, saying, *"The poor you have with you always"* (John 12:8).

On the other hand, you have other Christians who are like a one-trick pony. It seems all they want to talk about is money and prosperity. Some have even turned the church into what I consider to be a new age, self-help mechanism for personal advancement and the power of positive thinking.

Unfortunately, the carnage left over as a result of these schools of thought are the needy people in the pews. At the very basic level, many Christian congregants and their pastors struggle with embracing wealth-teaching and its proper application in the church.

In order for you to begin wealth building with the objective of kingdom building, your faith must be secure—and you should truly believe, not that you can, but also God wants you to.

Why struggle with the idea of whether or not God's covenant includes wealth building? It is written in the Book! Place your faith in the Word of God.

Many have bought into the erroneous theology which teaches that Jesus was poor, and we should follow His example.

Let's explore some of these issues.

IS CHRISTIAN POVERTY BIBLICAL?

Money, is an inanimate object and by default can not be inherently good or bad. Contrary to what many say, money doesn't change you; it may only bring to the surface what's already on the inside. If you are tight-fisted with a dollar, you'll most likely be the same with a million dollars. If you don't pay tithes on 50 cents, you won't pay it on 50 million. If you are arrogant, money will just give you the opportunity to spend, spend, spend, acquiring more to brag about.

Evidently, the Lord considers money a topic worth discussing or, as I mentioned earlier, He wouldn't have mentioned it so often in Scripture. Perhaps the question is, "How do we find the right balance concerning Christian faith and money?" And, "What does God's Word really say about the topic that will increase our faith for wealth?"

Let's start with what Jesus said: *"Blessed are the poor in spirit, for theirs is the kingdom of heaven"* (Matthew 5:3).

This is one of the scriptures that have caused certain Christians to sell everything they have, live in poverty, and serve the poor. While this sounds noble, it is an inaccurate interpretation.

Noted biblical scholar, A.T. Robertson, points out that the Greek word for "poor" used here, *ptochos,* means spiritual destitution. It is related to the word applied to the beggar Lazarus in Luke 16:20,22 (*ptosso*), which means to crouch or cower.[1] So to be "poor in spirit" has everything to do with one being spiritually broken and hurt, and in need of a healing—which Jesus promises. It has nothing to do with being financially impoverished.

Therefore, it is safe to say that one does not need to accept a life of poverty in order to be pleasing to God. In fact, if all believers were to do this, how would the church operate in perpetuity? It wouldn't; and the Gospel would not be financed in today's culture, where radio and television time as well as internet advertising are certainly not free. If we are not wealth building for kingdom building then we are missing an essential missional assignment of every believer.

WAS JESUS POOR?

I cringe when I hear arguments and false assumptions of Jesus being poor and lowly—implying that since He had no money we should live the same way. I have news for you. Jesus was not a pauper! He may not have been as affluent as the High Priests of His day, but He certainly was far removed from poverty. Any conclusion that Jesus was penniless simply lacks, biblical evidence. The best argument for His poverty can be made using 2 Corinthians 8:9 *"For you know the grace of our Lord Jesus Christ, that though He was rich, yet for your sakes He became poor, that you through His poverty might become rich."*

Here is the problem with this verse: if we say this is proof that Jesus was poor, then we must also accept it as evidence that this is a prosperity text which provides that all believers are made financially rich by coming to Christ.

In this passage Paul is speaking spiritually of Jesus' poverty—He, God, emptied Himself to walk in sinful flesh. From heaven's point of view our mortal beings are poor when compared to the Spirit. Therefore, by lowering Himself into our place, we are exalted to the richness of His glory. We can't have it both ways and use this text to speak to financial poverty and spiritual riches!

Another verse people refer to is Luke 9:58: *"And Jesus said to him, 'Foxes have holes and birds of the air have nests, but the Son of Man has nowhere to lay His head.'"*

As Bible scholar Richard C. H. Lenski notes, Jesus wanted to let an interested follower know that to join Him and His disciples, he would be given to an itinerant life, always on the move, with no fixed home to rest—just constantly doing ministry.[2]

Clearly, Jesus believed in giving all to spread the Gospel and walking in excellence, but in no way does this text prove He was some sort of beggar.

While many point to the fact God's Son was born in a manager, this does not give evidence of His financial poverty. Scripture simply states that Mary gave birth there because there was no room in the inn (Luke 2:7).

This is certainly no indication that Joseph couldn't afford a room for his pregnant wife. For example, just because *expedia.com* declines my reservation request does not mean I can't afford to stay at a hotel.

Moreover, how poor could Joseph have been?

- He certainly had enough money to travel with his family to Egypt and back by caravan (Matthew 2:13-19).
- He certainly had been compensated for being in the carpentry business (Matthew 13:55).
- He certainly had enough to pay for the annual family vacation to Jerusalem for Passover (Luke 2:41), plus put a roof over Jesus' head for the rest of the year.

So, at a minimum, Jesus did not grow up in poverty and was at least raised as middle class by standards of the time. Also, we must not forget the value of the gold, frankincense, and myrrh gifted to him at birth—which surely had considerable value.

Just before Jesus launched His public ministry, He worked in His father's business every day. As carpenters, Joseph and Son would have created farm tools (carts, plows, winnowing forks, and yokes), house parts (doors, frames, posts, and beams), furniture, and kitchen utensils.

These items would have certainly been in high demand. Moreover, Joseph must have been a well-known carpenter, since everyone in the entire region identified Jesus as his son (Matthew 13:55).

Jesus' ministry operated with economic stewardship—He even assigned Judas to what amounted to CFO duties after calling him as a disciple (John 13:29). You certainly don't need a person to manage your treasury if your not raising substantial amounts of money.

IS IT POSSIBLE TO BE RICH AND GO TO HEAVEN?

Another debatable scripture, is found in Mark 10:25: *"It is easier for a camel to go through the eye of a needle than for a rich man to enter the kingdom of God."* Many have interpreted this to mean that it is impossible for wealthy people to make it to heaven.

I repeat: if we are all financially destitute, whose tithes and offerings will finance the kingdom expansion? Are those who served God in Bible days (Abraham, David, Esther, Isaiah, Amos, etc.) doomed to hell because they amassed fortunes? Certainly not. If you view Mark 10:25 through the lens of the first half of the verse and not continue to the end, you might miss where Jesus makes clear His personal views on wealth and materialism.

Note that Jesus does not say it is difficult or impossible for rich people to go to heaven. He is answering the question, "How hard is it?"—clarifying that being wealthy is not an issue for Him; it is *trusting* in riches that is the concern, which we addressed in chapter 5.

The Lord has no problem with your power to get wealth, using your seed wisely, or anything else we have discussed in this book. However, wealth must have a purpose—I argue it is to build the kingdom.

The disciples' response is even more interesting. They questioned, *"Who then can be saved?"* (verse 26). In their thinking, *everyone* wants to be rich.

Jesus then states the material blessings we can expect for following Him. And we will receive them *"a hundredfold now in this time...and in the age to come, eternal life"* (verse 30). Eternity with Christ is the bonus!

While I wouldn't necessarily call Jesus a capitalist, both His cultural background as a Jew and His teachings, move me to believe He was a hard worker and entrepreneurial.

Clearly, wealth should not be all we strive for, but it should be part of our desire to live a better life now. There are two principles this text teaches us which we cannot ignore:

1. No man can be rich on earth and inherit the kingdom without God.
2. Wealth is not a sign of the divine, nor a guarantee.

CHRISTIAN FAITH AND WEALTH CAN WORK TOGETHER

Wealth is a valid part of the faith conversation. In this section, I am certainly taking license to use faith in the general sense of believing.

Christian faith can be seen woven throughout the fabric of our society; it is what characterized our ancestors. "In God we Trust" is more than just a slogan: I believe it is the identity of who all Americans are called to be.

Christian faith was crucial in shaping this nation's hope for independence and self-sufficiency.

It is no coincidence that in early America, most activity was centered on religious institutions. Judges were ministers, churches were schoolhouses, and our nation opened its arms as a haven of religious expression.

What we believe is the distinguishing factor between wealth accumulation and poverty: anchored by it, in our hearts we can boldly face the unknown with full confidence that we will succeed.

Your venture can't be undertaken, your dream fulfilled, or your task accomplished without faith. It is needed by all: families, entrepreneurs, employees, ministers, and politicians. A man or woman who walks in faith has something extra in their tank to help them go the distance in their pursuit of happiness.

THE DANGER OF FAITH INEQUALITY

The media has had a field day promoting income inequality as one of the great social ills of our time. While I agree the issue is troubling, I believe there is an even greater sickness in our society—*faith* inequality. I wish everyone the same measure of belief in God and His Word so that all could be equally blessed by it.

Even if you were to apply the principle of using your power to get wealth to start a business, one of the key differentiating factors between your venture and the next Christian's may be: who believes more? Who makes the mental and spiritual shift that enables them to live in abundance before it materializes?

While I was speaking of faith in a very general sense, now more specifically, I argue that true Christian faith rests on the power of Christ to form new realities and bring us into fresh possibilities.

As a follower of Jesus, I see faith as more than just believing. It is *knowing* that He cares about me, that

He desires the best for my life, and that His Word is something I can "take to the bank."

Unlike many, God never bounces a check! If His Word says I have been designed to create an enterprise for wealth building using the abilities He has given me so that I can finance the expansion of His kingdom, I wholeheartedly believe it. If He has created a cycle of wealth and is constantly sending me opportunities to enter this cycle, then I want to take advantage of them.

If you study our country's successful trail-blazers, you will find that it was not only money, intelligence, or good fortune that separated them from the pack—many mention the role of their Christian faith.

Jin Sook Chang, one of the founders of the women's apparel chain, *Forever 21*, speaks of how, in prayer, God told her to open a store and that she would be successful.

Her power to get wealth was identified and the entrance ramp of her cycle of wealth was provided; the only thing that could have held her back was a lack of faith. Thank the Lord, she believed!

The implications of faith as the key factor for wealth building cannot be underestimated.

FAITH IS THE CURRENCY OF A DIVINE TRANSACTION

Let's drill down on the faith element that sets the Father's promises for your wealth into motion.

The word "faith" appears 252 times in the New King James Version of the Bible. This tells me how significant it is in God's eyes.

Since Abraham is the "Father of Faith," and the first person in the Bible to be tagged as being *"very rich"* (Genesis 13:2), there is a biblical connection we need to discover about how faith and wealth truly operate. *"So what can we say that Abraham, the father of our people, learned about faith? If Abraham was made right by the things he did, he had a reason to brag. But this is not God's view, because the Scripture says, 'Abraham believed God, and God accepted Abraham's faith, and that faith made him right with God'"* (Romans 4:1-3 NCV).

There are two extremely important principles found in this passage that really distinguish Christian faith: First, by faith, Abraham believed God. Second, the Lord accepted his faith.

A divine transaction took place. It's almost as if two big pieces of a puzzle had to properly fit together —God held one and Abraham held the other.

Because Abraham's faith was the perfect size to fit God's hand, they came into agreement. This was only possible because of one major reason: Abraham believed God, even the promise about him becoming wealthy.

Abraham found success since he didn't try to use a wrong-shaped piece from another puzzle. He put the God-piece he was given into what was held by the Almighty. They were fully reconciled.

Here's what each of us need to understand. You

cannot simply "believe God" and then continue to do whatever you please, claiming the Lord's blessing somehow rests upon your stewardship of putting His Word to work. God can only accept faith that is based in biblical truth.

Donnie Smith, the CEO of Tyson Foods, states, *"My faith influences how I think, what I do, what I say. There are a lot of great biblical principles that are fundamental to operating a good business. Being fair and telling the truth are biblical principles."* [3]

If faith is something that must be accepted by God, then Mr. Smith's worldview is totally correct because it's biblical.

Faith is so much more than a positive, affirmative thought. The Lord doesn't buy into or acknowledge the psychobabble from the realm of "positive thinking."

Faith is not just conjuring up something we hope for; that's not biblically sound. To say we have trust and belief for the Lord to give us an answer that is not advantageous to our spiritual walk—or would draw us away from Him and not exalt His name in the earth—is definitely not faith. Also, to claim we have expectation for wealth, yet our heart is not inclined to use it for the expansion of His kingdom, is not true faith in the Word but positive or hopeful thinking.

God will not accept or bless what is not reflective of His truth.

Abraham and his descendants received a promise that the whole world would be theirs. That wealth guarantee did not come by the law or the Ten

Commandments, *"but through being right with God by his faith"* (Romans 4:13 NCV).

If man could be saved by completing a checklist of rules and regulations, there would have been no need for Jesus to die on a cross—there would be no reason to have faith.

I believe much of the frustration regarding personal finances, giving, and prosperity in the church today is attributable to a basic lack of understanding.

If faith is required, and must be accepted, then many people who are giving in church on a Sunday morning may be reducing their giving to nothing more than a lottery ticket. When you buy such a ticket, the best you can do is pray, cross your fingers, and hope you win. But I'm sure you have probably learned by now, that "giving" in this manner rarely, if ever, produces a return. In this sense, many misunderstand faith and confuse it with thinking and religious practice—and then they wonder why it's not working for them.

Without faith, you could give your tithe, but God would not *"open for you the windows of heaven and pour out for you such a blessing that there [would] not be room enough to receive it"* (Malachi 3:10). His promise is not tied to the practice of giving, but linked to the heart of the giver's trust and belief in the Bible.

If faith is not present, what I give will not be returned to me, *"good measure, pressed down, shaken together, and running over"* (Luke 6:38). Jesus continues this teaching by adding that the way we bless others is how God blesses us. This agreement falls apart if our motives are wrong. In other words, the transaction is voided in the Bank of Heaven.

God's response is based on what He sees as the purpose of your heart. The Lord knows if you are giving out of tradition, guilt, crowd dynamics, peer pressure, trying to strike it rich, or to make yourself look good in front of your friends.

Those transactions don't cut it with the Bank of Heaven. The only word the Lord is looking for on your deposit slip is *faith*.

IS YOUR FAITH PERSISTENT?

Some look at their financial circumstances and glibly say, "I'll just believe God." But their words ring hollow. It's like believing it might rain, yet you leave the house without taking an umbrella.

The Lord is not just looking for half-hearted belief, but *persistent* faith.

Jesus shared a story with His disciples about a judge who never gave God a thought and didn't really care about the people he had jurisdiction over. But there was a widow in the city who kept after him, pleading, "Please protect me! My rights are being violated!"

After ignoring her for quite some time, he thought, "She is a thorn in my flesh. I'd better do something about it, or this woman will never stop her pestering. Who knows? She might even attack me!"

Jesus made this point: *"Listen to what the unjust judge says. And will not God bring about justice for his chosen ones, who cry out to him day and night? Will he keep putting them off? I tell you, he will see that they get justice, and quickly. However, when the Son of Man comes, will he find faith on the earth?"* (Luke 18:6-8 NIV).

On this planet and at the gates of heaven, only faith will be accepted by God. Without it, you will not gain entrance to your earthly or eternal reward. Faith is the real secret supporting all the other secrets in this book. As Scripture clearly states: *"Without faith no one can please God"* (Hebrews 11:6 CEV).

Again, we come face to face with this divine principle: **the gifts of God are not self-centered possessions of a narcissist or an egomaniac.** Faith is not all about us; rather, it concerns pleasing our heavenly Father. Instead of focusing on the benefits or what we can extract for ourselves, it's time to look at what we are contributing to the kingdom and placing all of our trust in the *Blessor.*

PUTTING THESE SECRETS TO THE TEST

When I started my corporate career, I understood what I needed to do to rise through the ranks. After overcoming some challenges, I was quickly promoted, slated to become one of the fastest moving young executives in the company. In the late 90s, I was the worldwide product manager for a *Fortune 100* insurance company. Sixty-five offices worldwide reported in to me for my product lines. At the same time, my company purchased a smaller competitor, which offered similar types of products. Although it was an acquisition, it felt more like a merger because most of the top executives of the smaller company acquired the majority of our jobs while our executives were laterally promoted or downright demoted.

I remember managing a product line that had been losing money annually. In one year, I was able to turn it around from a 15 million dollar a year product loss leader to a 45 million dollar profit. That's a 30 million dollar swing! If I had received just 1% of that profit as a bonus, I would have been pretty happy. Instead, I received some restricted stock and a $10,000 bonus.

Wow! I figured if I was going to work that hard for someone else, I could do just as well for myself. Notice that "I" decided; I did not consider if God would accept this transaction and account it to faith.

Not wanting to deal with a demotion, I decided to explore other opportunities in the insurance industry. A competitor offered me one such possibility. After two years there, in the interest of polishing more of my entrepreneurial skills, I was given the chance to move from the underwriting side of insurance to the sales side at a growing brokerage firm headquartered in Manhattan, New York. I remember declaring how God had blessed me.

Well, that move didn't turn out so well. Within six months of working there, I regretted the decision. The senior management team was not committed to my product lines and we didn't see eye to eye for various reasons. So, I decided to leave, and it was a mutual parting.

I had made several hasty moves and assumed they were acceptable to God, since I was doing so in faith. Now sitting at home, unemployed, I became rather frustrated—wondering how I had traveled the road to unemployment. I had never faced corporate failure before and didn't know how to deal with it.

To be honest, I went through a period of depression. I was making decisions under the guise of faith that weren't acceptable to God. As I learned the hard way, this will usually lead to poor mental and spiritual health.

Fear wears many faces. How was I going to provide for my family? We had just moved into a new house, welcomed another baby, and the pressure and weight of the world were on me. My anger became so entrenched that I even felt that in some way God had abandoned me. I questioned, "What good is my faith if it has lead to this?"

One day I was in my prayer room. After making my petition to the Lord, I told Him that I wouldn't utter another word unless He spoke to me.

Suddenly, I heard the Lord say, "Are you finished yet?"

It was as if my heavenly Father was trying to get a *faith plan* through to me the whole time, but I was too busy moving by my own unacceptable faith. I had the wrong piece to God's puzzle.

Right after that moment, I repented for my accusations, surrendered everything totally to Him and replied, "Yes, Lord I'm ready to listen."

Shortly thereafter, I began to feel inspiration

spreading throughout my entire being. God told me to open up my own insurance brokerage firm—and He even gave me the name: Professional Risk Solutions.

Suddenly, everything fell into sharp focus. I was to put together all my underwriting skills, product knowledge, technical expertise, and the sales techniques I had developed.

What was I waiting for? When God speaks, it eclipses everything else.

From that day forward, my greatest challenge was to be persistent in believing what God had commanded. It was to *believe* wealthy and *be* wealthy.

In the fall of 2001, I launched the business out of my home. Within six months I hired my first assistant. Providing income for someone else was empowering. Three months later, I employed another person and we had to move into a small office space.

Terri and I kept putting works with our faith and God kept customers coming. We prayed like it was all up to God and worked like it was all up to us.

The momentum was unstoppable. We gained more clients and credibility in the marketplace. Before I knew it, I had achieved my five-year business plan in three years, and we continued to grow with a wonderful team. Soon we were opening up more offices—in Florida, Pennsylvania, and Maryland. We were being quoted in the media as "thought leaders."

From Professional Risk Solutions, I was able to launch other companies in real estate, fitness, and commercial cleaning services. I have also prospered as an angel investor in some successful early-stage enterprises.

By following God's instructions, like Abraham, I am not ashamed to say that I became financially wealthy. The Lord showed me the missing piece of the puzzle that He needed me to grab hold of—and I never let it go!

I constantly receive overtures to purchase my core business from some of the top financial service firms. There are days I wish I could say "yes," but the Lord has not yet released me.

Even if you feel like you have made some missteps in faith in the past, never quit. Like Abraham, give God the "acceptable" He demands. This is faith!

There is nothing unique about me. I'm not your summa cum laude, but an average student. In college, I did okay. I'm just a guy who finally stopped getting in his own way and decided to make God's dream for his life a reality by working it the best he could with the knowledge he had.

Has everything worked out perfectly? No. Did I have business ideas that fizzled? Absolutely. As others will attest to, you learn as much from your failures as you do from your successes.

No matter who you are, or at what level you operate, life is full of highs and lows:

- Trials and tribulations.
- Success and failures.
- Joys and pains.
- Health and sickness
- Wealth and poverty.

A Christian who is not firmly anchored in faith will be tossed around by winds of fear and waves of doubt. The journey of life can be long and tenuous, but with God as your partner, it is more than rewarding.

Remember these wealth building secrets:

- Christian poverty is not biblical.
- Jesus was not financially poor. He was at least middle class and perhaps inherited some wealth from His birth.
- In the divine transaction, we must believe God and He must accept our faith.
- Every gift of the Father is received through faith.
- God only accepts faith that is based on His truth.
- The Lord is looking for *persistent* faith.
- God's favor is to be experienced now and for eternity.

CHAPTER NOTES

Introduction
1. http://usatoday30.usatoday.com/sports/story/2012-04-22/Pro-athletes-and-financial-trouble/54465664/1
2. https://www.crownmoneymap.org/MoneyMap/SmallGroup/Downloads/2300ScriptureReferences_6_0 8.pdf

3. http://www.nj.com/politics/index.ssf/2013/09/
poverty_in_nj_reaches_52-year_high_new_
report_shows.html

Chapter 1:
1. http://www.forbes.com/sites/kerryadolan/2014/07/
08/how-the-stroh-family-lost-the-largest-private-beer-
fortune-in-the-u-s/

Chapter 3:
1. Stanley, Thomas J., and Danko, William D. *The Millionaire Next Door*, New York: Pocket Books, 1998, p. 3.
2. Gray, Farrah, with Harris, Fran. *Reallionaire: Nine Steps to Becoming Rich from the Inside Out*, Deerfield Beach, FL: Health Communications, Inc., p. 5.
3. Thomas J. Stanley and William D. Danko, *The Millionaire Next Door*, New York: Pocket Books, 1998.
4. NFIB, The Voice of Small Business, 411 Small Business Facts, "How many jobs does small business provide in the Unites States?" Available: http://www.411sbfacts.com/speeches.html#q3
5. U. S. Bureau of Labor Statistics, The Employment Situation: August 2009. Available: http://www.bls.gov/news.release/empsit.nr0.htm
6. U. S. Bureau of Labor Statistics. Available: ftp://ftp.bls.gov/pub/special.requests/lf/aat12.txt
7. Hansen, Mark Victor and Allen, Robert. *The One Minute Millionaire,* New York: Harmony Books, 2002, p.116.
8. Hagstrom, Robert G.; Miller, Bill; Fisher, Ken. *The Warren Buffet Way,* New York: John Wiley & Sons, 2004, p. 27.

Chapter 4:
  1. Schroeder, Alice, *The Snowball: Warren Buffet and the Business of Life*, New York: Bantam, 2008.

Chapter 6:
  1. http://www.theatlantic.com/business/archive/2014/03/are-the-suburbs-making-people-live-paycheck-to-paycheck/284586/

Chapter 7
  1. Robertson, A. T., *Word Pictures in the New Testament*. Nashville, TN: Broadman Press, 1933.
  2. Lenski, R. C. H., *The Interpretation of St. Luke's Gospel*. Minneapolis, MN: Augsburg Publishing House, 1961, p.560.

FOR ADDITIONAL RESOURCES
OR TO SCHEDULE THE AUTHOR FOR
SPEAKING ENGAGEMENTS, CONTACT:

DE'ANDRE SALTER
C/O THE TABERNACLE CHURCH
1253 NEW MARKET AVENUE
SOUTH PLAINFIELD, NJ 07080

PHONE: (908) 222-9990
EMAIL: booking@deandresalter.com
INTERNET: www.deandresalter.com